HOLLYWOOD GODDESSES

Rita Hayworth

HOLLYWOOD GODDESSES

How the stars were born – profiles of eighteen super-stars, the Hollywood Goddesses – from early struggles to ultimate success. Revealing text with pictures to match, in colour and black and white, and up-to-date filmographies.

Edited by Michael Jay

Galahad Books · New York

© 1982 Orbis Publishing Limited, London
Published by Galahad Books
95 Madison Avenue
New York, New York 10016

ISBN: 0-88365-630-2

Printed in Italy

Many of the illustrations come from stills issued to publicize films made or distributed by the following companies: Avco Embassy, Howard Hughes, Columbia, EMI, Hammer, IPC, Dino de Laurentiis, London Films, MGM, Mirisch, Paramount, Rank, Republic, RKO, David O. Selznick, Svenskfilm, Titanus, 20th Century-Fox, Ufa, United Artists, Universal, Warner Brothers. Although every effort is being made to trace the present copyright holders, we apologize in advance for any unintentional omission or neglect and will be pleased to insert the appropriate acknowledgment to companies or individuals in any subsequent edition of this publication.

Acknowledgments: Atmosphère, Joel Finler Collection, Ronald Grant Archive, Kobal Collection, Museum of Modern Art, New York, National Film Archive, David Robinson, Talisman Books, Bob Willoughby Collection.

CONTENTS

Ingrid Bergman
As time goes by

Discovered in Sweden in the early Thirties, Ingrid Bergman rose to the rank of international star in the Forties, proving herself a brilliant partner to Bogart, Cooper, Grant and Tracy. For many years the seductions of stardom left her unmoved and she never allowed herself to become stereotyped. Today, some fifty years on, and after a series of uneven films, she still commands respect and admiration throughout the industry

Far left: portrait of Bergman in 1942. Above left: her performance in På Solsidan *attracted the interest of the American press. Above: star of Selznick's* Intermezzo, *a virtual copy of the original Swedish film. Below: although Bergman's Broadway portrayal of Joan was a triumph, her screen role in* Joan of Arc *was not well received*

Filmography

1935 Munkbrogreven; Bränningar (USA: The Surf); Swedenhielms; Valborgsmässoafton. **'36** På Solsidan; Intermezzo. **'38** Dollar; Die 4 Gesellen (GER); En Kvinne Ansikte. **'39** En Enda Natt; Intermezzo: a Love Story (USA) (GB: Escape to Happiness). **'40** Juniatten. *All remaining films USA unless specified:* **'41** Adam Had Four Sons; Rage in Heaven; Dr Jekyll and Mr Hyde. **'42** Casablanca. **'43** Swedes in America (short) (GB: Ingrid Bergman Answers); For Whom the Bell Tolls; Saratoga Trunk. **'44** Gaslight (GB: The Murder in Thornton Square). **'45** The Bells of St Mary's; Spellbound. **'46** Notorious; The American Greed (short) (GB: American Brotherhood Week). **'48** Arch of Triumph; Joan of Arc. **'49** Under Capricorn (GB). **'50** Stromboli, Terra di Dio (IT) (USA: God's Land). **'51** Europa '51 (IT) (USA: The Greatest Love). **'53** Siamo Donne *ep* Il Pollo (IT) (USA: Five Women/of Life and Love *ep* Ingrid Bergman; GB: We Women/We, the Women). **'54** Viaggio in Italia (IT-FR) (USA: Strangers; GB: The Lonely Woman/Journey to Italy); Giovanna d'Arco al Rogo (IT-FR); Angst (GER-FR) (GB: Fear). **'56** Elena et les Hommes (FR-IT) (USA: Paris Does Strange Things; GB: The Night Does Strange Things); Anastasia (GB). **'58** Indiscreet (GB); The Inn of the Sixth Happiness (GB). **'59** The Camp (narr. only) (short). **'61** Goodbye Again (USA-FR). **'64** Der Besuch (GER-FR-IT) (USA: The Visit); The Yellow Rolls-Royce (GB); Stimulantia *ep* Smycket (SW). **'69** Cactus Flower. **'70** A Walk in the Spring Rain; Henri Langlois/Langlois (guest) (doc) (FR). **'73** From the Mixed-Up Files of Mrs Basil E. Frankweiler (GB: The Hideaways). **'74** Murder on the Orient Express (GB). **'76** A Matter of Time (USA-IT). **'78** Herbstsonate (GER) (USA: Autumn Sonata).

Born in Stockholm, Sweden, on August 29, 1915, Ingrid Bergman was brought up by her elderly uncle after the death of her parents, and at 17 joined Stockholm's Royal School of Dramatic Art where she was soon being chosen for the major roles. In 1933, she signed a contract with the Svenskfilmindustri and made her first screen appearance in *Munkbrogreven* (1935, The Count of the Monk's Bridge). By her fifth film, *På Solsidan* (1936, On the Sunny Side), she had become a star in Sweden. On this and several other occasions she worked under the direction of Gustaf Molander, who managed to bring out the full range of her talents.

Then, in 1939, David O. Selznick, to whom her growing reputation had been pointed out, brought her to Hollywood and cast her in the remake of *Intermezzo: a Love Story*, (she had already starred in the Swedish version) alongside Leslie Howard. Selznick, a great discoverer and modeller of actresses, was aware of the problems inherent in trying to 'sell' foreign stars to the American public, and astutely decided to place his bets on a fresh, natural and healthy image, relying on, in *Intermezzo*, the sort of story that he knew the public would accept. The gamble paid off and Bergman became an instant success in Hollywood.

However, after only a couple more roles as a pure and loyal woman, Bergman rebelled. Conscious of her potential, she refused to be typecast and fought for the part of Ivy, the barmaid of easy virtue, in Victor Fleming's *Dr Jekyll and Mr Hyde* (1941).

This complete role-change, however, served only to 'enrich' her screen image. Many of the subsequent Bergman heroines were two-faced and their moral irresolution made them fascinating to watch. This was true of *Saratoga Trunk* (1943), in which she played an illegitimate Creole adventuress in engaging manner, *Notorious* (1946), in which she was a lady of loose morals but admirable intentions, and *Under Capricorn* (1949), in which, while eloping, she murdered her brother who was following her. These films represent the 'black' aspect of her Hollywood character. The heroines are thrown into a booby-trapped, nightmarish world and their physical or mental degradation is all the more suggestive and convincing because the appearance of the actress seems to contradict it.

On the other hand *For Whom the Bell Tolls* (1943), *Spellbound*, *The Bells of St Mary's* (both 1945) and *Joan of Arc* (1948) – all roles in which she was taking a stand – summarize the positive aspect of the Bergman character. They highlight her idealism, her sincerity and altruism, all of which Selznick had been sensitive to. And yet the ambiguous Bergman characters are preferable to her rather 'toneless' and angelic presentations. In *Casablanca* (1942), the pull of two men, Rick Blaine (Humphrey Bogart) and Victor Laszlo (Paul Henreid), unearths a shaky division of loyalties – on the one hand there is her husband and on the other her commitment to the past.

In spite of the diversity of the studios she worked for and the types of characters she played, Bergman's American career retained a certain unity through the influence of the ever-present Selznick, whose contradictory tastes enabled him to create icy neurotics, fading madonnas and nymphomaniacs. After the break with Selznick in 1946 something was definitely lost from Bergman's style, and nothing new appeared to take its place.

The man who had finally persuaded her to make the break from Selznick was Peter Lindstrom, a Swedish dentist to whom Bergman had been married since the beginning of her career. His intelligent advice in Sweden became sadly misguided in Hollywood. *Arch of Triumph* (1948) sustained considerable losses. In the same year, Bergman saw Roberto Rossellini's *Roma, Città Aperta* (*Rome, Open City*) and, greatly impressed, wrote to him

offering her services.

Curiously, films of the Rossellini period in the Fifties, in spite of some complex narratives, were not so much a denial of the 'Bergman myth' of virginal purity than a change in its essential qualities. *Stromboli* (1950, *God's Land*), was slightly exceptional in that it still partly stemmed from Rossellini's earlier neo-realistic style. Bergman played an unhappy wife escaping from the island of the title. However, all her later films in Italy formed a link with her earlier American films. The temptations of sainthood in *Europa '51* (1951, *The Greatest Love*) are reminiscent of the religious inspiration of *The Bells of St Mary's* and *Joan of Arc*; and the marital hell in *Stromboli* harks back to the tormented wife in *Gaslight* (1944, *The Murder in Thornton Square*) – the film for which she won her first Academy Award, playing a woman blindly in love with a contemptible adventurer. But the more naturalistic approach of Rossellini was not compatible with either actress or theme. In 1950 Bergman finally divorced Lindstrom and married Rossellini, thereby legalizing a relationship that had caused a public outcry against her 'scandalous' behaviour and seriously damaged her career prospects in Hollywood. But when the strain of a series of unsuccessful films proved too much and Bergman decided to return to the stage for a while, Rossellini went to make a film in India and returned with the wife of an Indian director. In 1957, with another divorce, the 'Rossellini period' was over.

20th Century-Fox had offered her the chance of an international comeback with *Anastasia* in 1956, a story about the escape of the Tsar's daughter in 1918. It was a tremendous success, winning Bergman her second Academy Award. There followed a series of roles devised to regain her internationally popular image. In *Anastasia*, *Indiscreet* (1958, again teamed with Cary Grant) and *Inn of the Sixth Happiness* (1958, as a missionary in China), Bergman achieved respectability. Several later films, of which *A Walk in the Spring Rain* (1970) – an intimate composition in half tones, about the affair of a married and middle-aged woman – was no exception, were not suitable material and did not allow her to attain her true potential, but in 1974 she won another Academy Award, this for Best Supporting Actress, in *Murder on the Orient Express* in which she played a timid and devout missionary.

In 1978, Bergman was cast in *Autumn Sonata* as the self-obsessed mother who is totally involved in her career– the first role worthy of her since the end of the Selznick period. She bravely exposed herself to Ingmar

Above left: Bergman and Bogart, the ill-fated lovers in Casablanca. *Above: in* The Yellow Rolls-Royce, *with Omar Sharif and Joyce Grenfell, Bergman, as a widow crossing war-torn Yugoslavia, outshone in an improbable plot. Below: a lady with a guilty secret in* Murder on the Orient Express

Bergman's scrutinizing eye and achieved, with his complicity, a character of great depth and nuance; this was probably one of the most complete, moving and intelligent creations of the actress' career.

Throughout her years in the cinema, she has maintained regular contact with the stage, playing in about ten plays between 1940 and 1967, including *Joan of Lorraine* (1946), for which she was awarded the Tony Award, *Tea and Sympathy* (1956), *Hedda Gabler* (1962), and *A Month in the Country* (1965), directed by Sir Michael Redgrave at the Yvonne Arnaud theatre in Guildford. In 1958 she married a theatrical impresario, Lars Schmidt.

Ingrid Bergman's career spans a remarkable number of years; they divide into four distinct periods – Sweden, Hollywood, Rossellini and the International period. She survived the disappearance of the Hollywood studios and the Rossellini experience. She also emerged well from several miscasts, thanks to her adaptability and to a thorough discipline that even her least interesting roles exhibit. She remains a combination of femininity, distance, honour and vulnerability, that still seduces us.

OLIVIER EYQUEM

Joan Crawford
Self-made Star

Joan Crawford was nothing if not a star. Others might have had more varied acting abilities, have sung and danced better, have been more statuesquely beautiful or sweetly pretty or unashamedly sexy, but they lacked Joan Crawford's naked will to stardom. Like the characters she played in so many of her films, she fought her way up from the bottom; she modelled and remodelled herself tirelessly to match changes of taste and fashion, she built her own personality, polished her party manners, refined her dress sense and became a lady. She learned how to act – surprisingly well – and, more importantly, to know and abide by her own limitations. And she worked: morning, noon and night; she was totally the star, living for her public and her fame.

In other words, she was every shop-girl's dream come true. The secret of her appeal lay in her apparent ordinariness. However hard a girl tried, however far she stretched her imagination, she could never really be a Garbo or a Dietrich; but she could, conceivably, be a Joan Crawford. If simple little Lucille LeSueur (Crawford's real name) from San Antonio, Texas, could become the biggest thing in Hollywood, then so could anyone. Or that, at least, was the easy fantasy.

Jazz-baby Joan
When Joan Crawford first really became that magic being, a star, she had already made at least 19 films. Discovered as a chorus girl in a Broadway show called *Innocent Eyes* she began her film career as an anonymous double for Norma Shearer. She worked her way up through bit parts to female lead in low-budget films, or played opposite male stars, such as Harry Langdon in *Tramp, Tramp, Tramp* (1926), or Lon Chaney in *The Unknown* (1927), who were important enough not to need a real co-star. With *Our Dancing Daughters* (1928), however, the die was cast; she was flaming youth, a jazz-baby who lived life to the full without caring for the consequences (until, of course, bitter experience made her care). She was also a star. She was 24 years old (most probably: ten years later her official birthdate was abruptly changed from 1904 to 1908), under contract to MGM for three years and well on the way to becoming a complete product of the studio system. In later years, when it became fashionable for stars and ex-stars to complain about their 'slavery' and the autocratic rule of Louis B. Mayer, she always stoutly defended Mayer as an understanding father-figure and captain of a generally happy ship.

Above: Joan keeps a close watch on what the fan magazines are saying about her. Her intense relationship with her fans began in the Twenties when MGM organized a competition to find a new name for their starlet Lucille LeSueuer – Joan Crawford was the result. Top and above left: George Hurrell's striking portraits helped her to win forceful roles

Movie mannequin
All the same, she was ambitious and had ideas of her own. She became increasingly conscious of the rough edges in her manners and personality, for which she blamed her humble background (when she left home to go on the stage, her mother, twice divorced, was working in a laundry), and set out to 'improve' herself. She began dating Douglas Fairbanks Jr and then, despite some parental objections, married him. She began moving in the smartest social circles around Pickfair, the home of Fairbanks Sr and his wife Mary Pickford, and she learned quickly. At work, too, she was learning and planning. She toyed with various images (for a while in 1930 she looked alarmingly like Jean Harlow, her hair briefly platinum blonde), before setting on the look which became her trade mark: the broad, full mouth

emphasized with heavy lipstick; the eyes – her best feature – madeup to look even larger than they were; the rest of her face became a boldly sculpted classical mask. She persuaded George Hurrell, the leading studio photographer, to take a series of striking pictures of her, virtually without makeup, to prove to the studio bosses that she could be convincing in strong melodramatic roles. She persuaded

As Sadie Thompson in Rain *(above) her appearance was termed 'bizarre'. Joan was more at ease as a hopeful show girl in* Dancing Lady *(above right) co-starring Clark Gable. By the Forties, she had matured into an actress of great power. Both* A Woman's Face *(right) and* Strange Cargo *(below right) provided her with strong roles;* Mildred Pierce *(below) won her an Oscar. In this scene she is falsely confessing to the murder of her husband to save the real culprit – her daughter who had killed him in a jealous rage*

Adrian, chief designer at the studio, to design a complete wardrobe for her. He particularly stressed her broad, square shoulders; soon, all across the USA women were copying her.

And so emerged a new 'mature' Joan, ready to play meaty roles in films like *Paid* (1930), in which she is imprisoned for a crime she did not commit and sets out to get even; and *Letty Lynton* (1932), where she is not imprisoned for a crime she *did* commit (poisoning an insanely ardent lover) and somehow manages to live happily ever after. Best of all was *Grand Hotel* (1932), in which she was genuinely touching as the hotel stenographer Flaemmchen – and managed to steal the picture right away from Garbo, a couple of Barrymores and others of similar standing.

Rain (1932), directed by Lewis Milestone at United Artists, was a mistake, since Sadie Thompson was a role which needed more than poise and personality to play, but she seldom made such a mistake again. From 1933 onwards her films were generally vehicles for her, and very sleek, finely tuned vehicles at that. True, she seemed in danger of becoming little more than a clothes-horse in some of them – but what a clothes-horse, and what clothes!

In film after film at this period – *Today We Live* (1933), *Chained, Forsaking All Others* (both 1934), *Love on the Run* (1936), *The Bride Wore Red* (1937) – she had nothing much to do except look gorgeous while two or three or more of the most eligible men in Hollywood fought for her favours. Often it was Clark Gable who finally won them. For good reasons she nearly always played modern roles – when she tried a period role in *The Gorgeous Hussy* (1936) critics immediately noted that 'century-old costumes do not go well with the pronounced modernity of her personality'. And indeed, through all her various incarnations, she did seem to belong unmistakably to the twentieth century: Aldous Huxley once said that she looked like a still-unnamed Dupont product. In 1938 she was pronounced 'box-office poison' – along with, admittedly, most of the biggest stars of the time – but no one seems to have bothered very much and she forged on into the Forties as hardly-disputed queen of MGM.

Her crown's awry

But her films were getting odder, as though behind the scenes nobody knew quite what to do with her. In 1935 you would have known exactly what to expect from a Crawford film; by 1940 it was almost impossible to guess – and this is a very alarming situation for a star, a real star, to be in, since it is consistency above all that counts. There could hardly be a more assorted group of films than *The Shining Hour* (1938), about a nightclub dancer who marries into a family of society neurotics; *The Ice Follies of 1939* (1939); *The Women* (1939), in which a society woman outmanoeuvres an ambitious shop-girl to keep the love of her (unseen) husband; *Strange Cargo* (1940), the story of a dance-hall girl who joins a band of convicts escaping from a French penal colony in the tropics; *Susan and God* (1940), a sophisticated comedy-drama about a nitwitted society woman who tries to convert her family and friends to a cranky religious movement; and *A Woman's Face* (1941), in which a hideously scarred criminal becomes converted to love and virtue after an operation on her face. Crawford is, in fact, very good in several of them – particularly *The Women*, where she

turns in a marvellously unsparing portrait of a vicious schemer – but it was becoming evident that her rule at MGM must be nearing its end, and that making a graceful transition to middle age might prove to be a problem for her.

A couple more films, and she left MGM, in her own words, 'by the back door'. She was put under contract to Warner Brothers, who brought her in perhaps as a handy rival to keep their top female star, Bette Davis, in line. They could not come up with a suitable property for her, and, apart from one brief guest appearance, she did not work for two years.

Then, in 1945, came *Mildred Pierce* which

gained her an Academy Award and revitalized her career. In *Mildred Pierce* she was still glamorous and sexually desirable, but, at the same time, old enough to have a troublesome teenage daughter and so suffer the pangs of despised mother-love as well. She had all the qualities for agonizing in the grand manner. In this and her next pictures – *Humoresque* (1946), *Possessed* (1947), *Flamingo Road* (1949) and *The Damned Don't Cry* (1950) – she might play a bitch, but always a somewhat sympathetic one: you knew what had made her that way, and suffered along with her. She had usually been born on the wrong side of the tracks, made her own way to the top by baking pies or building empires for her menfolk, and then found that luxury and glamour were vain without the love of a good man (or a good child, or both) – a secretly satisfying conclu-

Above: Crawford gave a superb performance in Humoresque *playing a rich socialite desperate for the love of a violinist (John Garfield) but incapable of coping with it. Right: as Vienna, a tough saloon owner in* Johnny Guitar, *she successfully fought a duel to the death. Below: one of her last parts – as a circus owner in* Berserk! *(1967)*

sion for those of her audience who might aspire to such wealthy heights but were unlikely ever to attain them.

She had assumed such a powerful – some would say overpowering – persona by this time that few of the shrinking, malleable men in her films could stand up to her: these were 'women's pictures' *par excellence*, products of an era when film-going was still the major spare-time occupation of the American public and a large proportion of this vast audience was female. Women generally either went by themselves to matinées or decided what their boyfriends or husbands should take them to. As television began to threaten this state of affairs, the audiences for Crawford's films began to tail off.

A tough and ruthless thriller, *Sudden Fear* (1952), gave her career another shot in the arm, and then she was back at MGM with *Torch Song* (1953) – starring in a musical, of all things, and showing that she still had fabulous

legs. She then made a series of disastrous films: shooting it out with Mercedes McCambridge at the end of *Johnny Guitar* (1954), Crawford's first and only Western; being threatened with murder by another woman (what man would dare?) in *Female on the Beach* (1955); and getting a typewriter thrown at her by a young psychopath in *Autumn Leaves* (1956).

After that came an apotheosis of a sort with *What Ever Happened to Baby Jane?* (1962), in which she starred with her old arch-rival Bette Davis as one of two sisters, both Hollywood has-beens, in a gleefully Grand Guignol piece. It was her last film of note: afterwards, she refused to take parts that suited her age, thereby missing many mature roles that she could have played very well. Instead she was confined to incidental parts in big films and leading roles in ever more tatty shockers, after the last of which, *Trog* (1970), she retired to concentrate on public relations for Pepsi-Cola, for which her fourth and final husband, Alfred Steele, had been an important executive.

Very much a recluse by the end of her life, she died in New York in 1977 – one of the last stars from an era when they really had faces.

The camera and Crawford

What more did she have than a face? A lot more acting talent than she has ever been given credit for. Apart from rare aberrations like *Rain*, her performances really do not date. Compared with Norma Shearer her greatest rival at MGM during the Thirties, Crawford comes live off the screen – however foolish the context – and Shearer does not. Bette Davis, Crawford's great rival at a later stage. could be wonderful with the right role and the right director. but without one or the other she is often mannered to the point of absurdity. Crawford is simpler, more direct in style, and absolutely consistent.

But then acting ability has little to do with star quality. Joan Crawford loved the camera so much that it just had to love her back. It fulfilled for her every childhood dream just as she did. vicariously but vividly, for millions of women in one-horse towns and anonymous cities all over the USA. After her very earliest days she was never much of a pin-up star for men: she was a woman's star, and especially an American star, who lived out a series of specifically American women's dreams. Vibrant, glamorous, self-made and self-sufficient. Joan Crawford was not so much *a* star as *the* star – the perfect summary of just what Hollywood in its heyday was all about.

JOHN RUSSELL TAYLOR

Filmography

1925 Lady of the Night (double for Norma Shearer); 'Miss MGM' (short); Proud Flesh; Pretty Ladies; The Only Thing; Old Clothes; Sally. Irene and Mary. **'26** Tramp. Tramp. Tramp; The Boob (GB: The Yokel); Paris (GB: Shadows of Paris). **'27** Winners of the Wilderness; The Taxi Dancer; The Understanding Heart; The Unknown; Twelve Miles Out; Spring Fever; West Point (GB: Eternal Youth). **'28** The Law of the Range; Rose-Marie; Across to Singapore; Four Walls; Our Dancing Daughters; Dream of Love. **'29** The Duke Steps Out; The Hollywood Revue of 1929; Our Modern Maidens; Untamed. **'30** Montana Moon; Our Blushing Brides; Paid/Within the Law. **'31** Dance. Fools. Dance; Laughing Sinners; This Modern Age; Possessed. **'32** The Stolen Jools (GB: The Slippery Pearls) (short) (guest); Grand Hotel; Letty Lynton; Rain. **'33** Today We Live; Dancing Lady. **'34** Sadie McKee; Chained; Forsaking All Others. **'35** No More Ladies; I Live My Life. **'36** The Gorgeous Hussy; Love on the Run; Screen Snapshots No 12 (short). **'37** Parnell (guest); The Last of Mrs Cheyney; The Bride Wore Red; Mannequin. **'38** The Shining Hour. **'39** The Ice Follies of 1939; The Women. **'40** Strange Cargo; Susan and God (GB: The Gay Mrs Trexal). **'41** A Woman's Face; When Ladies Meet. **'42** They All Kissed the Bride; Reunion/Reunion in France (GB: Mademoiselle France). **'43** Above Suspicion; For Men Only (short). **'44** Hollywood Canteen (guest). **'45** Mildred Pierce. **'46** Humoresque. **'47** Possessed; Daisy Kenyon. **'49** Flamingo Road; It's a Great Feeling (guest). **'50** The Damned Don't Cry; Harriet Craig. **'51** Goodbye, My Fancy. **'52** This Woman is Dangerous; Sudden Fear. **'53** Torch Song. **'54** Johnny Guitar. **'55** Female on the Beach; Queen Bee. **'56** Autumn Leaves. **'57** The Story of Esther Costello (GB); The Best of Everything. **'62** What Ever Happened to Baby Jane? **'63** The Caretakers (GB: Borderlines); Strait-Jacket. **'65** I Saw What You Did. **'67** Berserk! (GB). **'70** Trog (GB).

All About Bette

'What a fool I was to come to Hollywood where they only understand platinum blondes and where legs are more important than talent'

On December 3, 1930, Bette Davis arrived in Hollywood. Originally from Lowell, Massachusetts (she was born in 1903), she had studied drama at the John Murray Anderson school, acting in summer repertory. She had won a modest but growing reputation as a promising young actress in two Broadway plays – *Broken Dishes* and *Solid South* – and had come to the attention of Universal studios, who put her under contract.

It was hardly an auspicious time for someone like Davis to break into films; she was pretty enough, in an odd way, but hardly fitted any of the moulds by which either the studios or the public judged beauty. The fact that she was, or wanted to be, a serious actress was irrelevant, if not actually a handicap to success. When she got off the train, no-one from the studio was there to meet her. In fact, a representative *had* been at the station but later reported that he had seen 'no-one who looked like an actress.' When head of the studio Carl Laemmle saw the first film in which she was cast, *Bad Sister* (1931), he said, 'Can you picture some poor guy going through hell and high water in a picture and ending up with *her* at the fade-out?'

Five undistinguished films later, Universal dropped her contract. Just as she and her

Above: even in publicity portraits Bette Davis avoided the glamorous extravagances of most other Hollywood actresses. Right: The Man Who Played God *provided her with a prestigious role as the fiancée of a concert pianist (George Arliss)*

mother were packing to return to New York and the theatre, George Arliss, then a leading star at Warner Brothers telephoned. A friend of his, Murray Kinnell, had worked with Davis in her fifth film *The Menace* (1932) and had thought she might be right for Arliss' upcoming *The Man Who Played God* (1932). In his autobiography, Arliss recalled:

'I did not expect anything but a nice little performance. But . . . the nice little part became a deep and vivid creation . . . I got from her a flash that illuminated mere words and inspired them with passion and emotion. That is the kind of light that cannot be hidden under a bushel.'

Warners, however, either didn't see that light, or didn't care; she was put under contract, but given a series of roles in mediocre pictures which today have few, if any, redeeming qualities except Davis' presence.

She was, of course, noticed by critics and the public, and her reputation as a solid actress continued to grow. She was a convincing vixen in *Cabin in the Cotton* (1932), and man-

aged to make even the most ludicrous Southern dialogue – 'Ah'd luv ta kiss yo, but ah jes washed mah hayuh' – sound believable. She fought with director Archie Mayo over the way she should play her mad scene in *Bordertown* (1935); she won, as she often did in battles with directors, and was proved right, as she often was in such cases, when the film was well received. Critics pointed to the subtlety of her portrayal of 'a fiery-souled, half-witted, love-crazed woman' (*Film Weekly*) in their reviews.

Davis has claimed that 'There wasn't one of my best pictures I didn't have to fight to get.' *Of Human Bondage* (1934), from the novel by Somerset Maugham, was one of the first. Director John Cromwell wanted her for the role of Mildred, a scheming waitress who ensnares a sensitive medical student, but Warners was reluctant to loan her to RKO for the film. Bette hounded Jack Warner every day for six months, and he finally gave in simply to be left in peace. She recalled in her autobiography *The Lonely Life*:

'My employers believed I would hang myself playing such an unpleasant heroine . . . I think they identified me with the character and felt we deserved each other.'

It is, seen now, perhaps not one of Davis' best performances; her Mildred is so constantly overwrought and nasty that one begins to wonder what even the obsessed student Philip Carey (Leslie Howard) could see in her. Put in historical perspective, however, the performance is both effective and courageous; at a time when 'movie star' meant glamour and sympathy, Davis had dared to look terrible and to be unsympathetic. All were surprised when

she was not even nominated for an Academy Award. When she won an Oscar for *Dangerous* (1935), she claimed it was given her because she had been overlooked the previous year.

In spite of the acclaim she received for *Of Human Bondage*, Warners threw her into five melodramas of variable quality before giving her the script of *Dangerous*. Davis says that she thought it 'maudlin and mawkish, with a pretense at quality', and that she had to work hard to make something of her role as an alcoholic actress bent on self-destruction. She is undoubtedly right about the screenplay, but she gives a performance of such intensity that one overlooks everything that is going on around her on screen.

Those critics who had begun to complain that she was fast developing a set of mannerisms and was playing too broadly for the screen were suprised at her tender and restrained Gaby in *The Petrified Forest* (1936). Yet, in spite of her obvious power at the box-office and her critical standing as a serious actress, Warners insisted that she make an empty comedy, *The Golden Arrow* (1936), and a flat and confused version of Dashiell Hammett's *The Maltese Falcon* called *Satan Met a Lady* (1936). Davis was understandably angry. To preserve her self-respect and her popularity, she wanted to make fewer films each year and to act only in those with scripts she thought intelligent. Warners reply was to cast her in something called *God's Country and the Woman* (made in 1936 with Beverley Roberts as the female lead), with the promise that if she made it she could have the part of Scarlett O'Hara in *Gone With the Wind* (1939). She refused and the studio put her on suspen-

Left: a role Davis fought to get – Mildred in Of Human Bondage, *co-starring Leslie Howard. Centre: Davis (with Miriam Hopkins) in* The Old Maid *– a study of repressed love. Top left:* Dark Victory *was one of her strongest melodramas; Humphrey Bogart played a minor part. Top: as the rich flirt Madge, she bewitched her father's employee Marvin (Richard Barthelmess) in* Cabin in the Cotton

sion for three months. She held out, refusing two other scripts offered her, with the comment 'If I continue to appear in mediocre pictures, I'll have no career worth fighting for'.

With the Davis–Warners feud at an impasse, Ludovico Toeplitz, who produced films in England, offered her a two-picture contract at £20,000 for each film, with script approval. She signed, but upon her arrival in London found herself under injunction from Warners. They claimed that she was contracted to work exclusively for that studio and was not allowed to make films for others. The entire film industry watched the ensuing court battle (which all actors applauded) as the outcome would determine how the studio system would work in the future. Davis lost her suit and was forced to return to Warners or to give up films until her long-term contract expired – but she

---

'I have never known the great actor who . . . didn't plan eventually to direct or produce. If he has no such dream, he is usually bitter, ungratified and eventually alcoholic'

---

did not lose out in the long run. Warners paid her legal fees and began to take her more seriously; the standard of her material temporarily rose.

Her first film upon her return to Hollywood was *Marked Woman* (1937), an above-average social-problem (prostitution) film which gave her a chance to show a wider range of emotion than usual. *Jezebel* (1938) began a long series of films specially tailored for Davis. They were for the most part what was then called 'women's pictures', melodramatic soap operas turning on romantic conflict and sacrifice. It would be a mistake, however, to dismiss them in the

light of the wider freedom of expression allowed in today's films. In the Thirties and Forties such films were taken seriously and accorded more than a little respect. The best of them attempted to illuminate areas of emotion, sexuality and human situation which could not be portrayed on the screen at that time in any other way. Those that Davis made were certainly among the best – she continuously fought for a certain level of intelligence in plot and dialogue, and insisted on as much realism as possible in her portrayals of disturbed or troubled women.

In *Jezebel* she was convincing as a wilful Southern belle who is made to suffer for her own strange peversity. In *Dark Victory* (1939) she alone lifted a maudlin tale of a woman slowly dying into an illuminating study of human understanding and sacrifice. In *Now*

Voyager (1942) she made a repressed spinster's transformation into a compassionate, mature woman believable and moving.

In 1946 she decided to set up her own production company with the films thus made to be released through Warners. A single film came from her company – *A Stolen Life* (1946) in which she played twins, one good, one evil, both in love with the same man. She found she was uncomfortable in the role of producer: 'I never really *produced*,' she said, 'I simply meddled as usual. If that was producing, I had been a mogul for years.'

From 1946 onward, Davis seemed to have a problem finding suitable material, and her popularity began to slip. *Winter Meeting* (1948) is a talky film about a poetess meeting a naval

Left: Bette with William Dix in The Nanny, *one of her best later roles. Above left: Her performance as stage star Margo Channing (here with Celeste Holm and Hugh Marlowe) helped* All About Eve *achieve a record of 14 Academy Award nominations (it won six). Above: Davis in full regalia as* The Virgin Queen *– her second portryal of Elizabeth the First*

officer who wants to be a priest. *Beyond the Forest* (1949) was forced upon her by Warners in spite of her warning that 'I'm too old and too strong for that part'. The film was savaged by the critics and the public stayed away. Nonetheless, it is one of the most enjoyable bad movies ever made. ('There never was a woman like Rosa Moline, a twelve-o'clock girl in a nine-o'clock town.') Davis pulls out all the stops and turns in one of the finest Bette Davis caricatures ever seen. She asked for her release from the studio and got it, although Jack Warner was considering her for Blanche in *A Streetcar Named Desire* (later made in 1951).

She was completing a rather ordinary melodrama about divorce, *Payment on Demand* (1951) at RKO, when she was offered the part of ageing actress Margo Channing in *All About Eve* (1950). Davis later recalled:

'I can think of no project that from the outset was as rewarding from the first day to the last . . . It was a great script, had a great director, and a cast of professionals all with parts they liked . . . After the picture was released I told Joe [Mankiewicz, the director] he had resurrected me from the dead.'

Davis was never better in a role that allowed

'There was more good acting at Hollywood parties than ever appeared on the screen'

---

her to play an actress larger than life, and at the same time to reveal the self-pity and vulnerability beneath. But this upswing in her career was not maintained; throughout the decade she was cast in poor roles.

Still, as had happened with *All About Eve*, a film came along which once more revitalized her career: Robert Aldrich's *What Ever Happened to Baby Jane?* (1962). She obviously more than enjoyed playing 'Grand Guignol', and the film was overwhelmingly popular everwhere in the world. Perhaps the one unfortunate aspect of its success was that, in spite of minor

Left: Bette became one of the murderer's victims in the whodunnit Death on the Nile. *Above: as the crazy, former child star in* What Ever Happened to Baby Jane? *she slowly destroyed her crippled sister*

---

forays back into 'women's films' such as *Where Love Has Gone* (1964), she was offered and accepted a series of ghoulish roles in progressively worse movies.

Davis' most notable recent achievement was an Emmy award for the TV series *Strangers: the Story of a Mother and Daughter*. She also tours the lecture circuit with her older films, and remains the determined figure she always was:

'I'll never make the mistake of saying I'm retired. You do that and you're finished. You just have to make sure you play older and older parts. Hell, I could do a million of those character roles. But I'm stubborn about playing the lead. I'd like to go out with my name above the title.'

She is still known as 'the finest actress of the American cinema'. There are those who have disputed that she acted at all, maintaining that all the characters she played were drowned by her own strong personality. It is a moot point, depending upon one's standards and definition of screen acting, although one could reply that she has played the widest range of roles in the widest range of mood of any actress ever to work in American films. Whatever the final judgment of her abilities as an actress, however, it cannot be denied that, whatever she does on the screen, it is impossible to take one's fascinated eyes off her.   DAVID OVERBEY

Quotations from The Lonely Life, *by Bette Davis (New York, G.P. Putnam's Sons, 1962)*

Filmography

1931 Bad Sister; Seed; Waterloo Bridge; Way Back Home (GB: Old Greatheart). **'32** The Menace; Hell's House (reissued as: Juvenile Court); The Man Who Played God (GB: The Silent Voice); So Big; The Rich Are Always With Us; The Dark Horse; Cabin in the Cotton; Three on a Match. **'33** 20,000 Years in Sing Sing; Parachute Jumper; Ex-Lady; The Working Man; Bureau of Missing Persons. **'34** The Big Shakedown; Fashions of 1934 (GB: Fashion Follies of 1934; USA retitling for TV: Fashions); Jimmy the Gent; Fog Over Frisco; Of Human Bondage; Housewife. **'35** Bordertown; The Girl From 10th Avenue (GB: Men on Her Mind); Front Page Woman; Special Agent; Dangerous. **'36** The Petrified Forest; The Golden Arrow; Satan Met a Lady. **'37** Marked Woman; Kid Galahad (USA retitling for TV: The Battling Bellhop); That Certain Woman; It's Love I'm After. **'38** Jezebel; The Sisters. **'39** Dark Victory; Juarez; The Old Maid; The Private Lives of Elizabeth and Essex. **'40** All This and Heaven Too; The Letter. **'41** the Great Lie; Shining Victory (uncredited guest); The Bride Came COD; The Little Foxes; The Man Who Came to Dinner. **'42** In This Our Life; Now, Voyager. **'43** Watch on the Rhine; Thank Your Lucky Stars; Old Aquaintance. **'44** Mr Skeffington; Hollywood Canteen. **'45** The Corn is Green. **'46** A Stolen Life; Deception. **'48** Winter Meeting; June Bride. **'49** Beyond the Forest. **'50** All About Eve. **'51** Payment on Demand; Another Man's Poison (GB). **'52** Phone Call From a Stranger; The Star. **'55** The Virgin Queen. **'56** The Catered Affair (GB: Wedding Breakfast); Storm Center. **'59** John Paul Jones; The Scapegoat (GB). **'61** Pocketful of Miracles. **'62** What Ever Happened to Baby Jane? **'63** La Noia (IT). **'64** Dead Ringer (GB: Dead Image); Where Love Has Gone; Hush . . . Hush, Sweet Charlotte. **'65** The Nanny (GB). **'67** The Anniversary (GB). **'69** Connecting Rooms (GB). **'71** Bunny O'Hare. **'72** Lo Scopone Scientifico (IT) (USA: The Scientific Cardplayer). **'76** Burnt Offerings. **'78** Return From Witch Mountain; Death on the Nile (GB).

Marlene
Dietrich

'One sees what one wants to see,'
said Josef von Sternberg, 'and I gave her nothing
that she did not already have.'

The Blue Angel

Josef von Sternberg described his first film with Dietrich as 'a celluloid monument to her'. It certainly made her a star.

The Blue Angel is the story of an elderly, respected school professor who becomes obsessed with a cabaret singer at the Blue Angel nightclub. Sacked from the school after being seduced by Lola-Lola, he marries her and becomes a clown in her travelling troupe. When it visits his old town he is painfully humiliated and, looking for solace, finds instead Lola with her new lover. Cast out, the pathetic figure wanders to his former classroom and dies there alone.

In Sternberg's cruellest study of sexual desire, Dietrich was teasingly provocative as the heartless Lola, stealing most of the scenes as she huskily sings 'Falling in Love Again' and 'I'm Naughty Little Lola', and bares her legs to Emil Jannings' professor. Heinrich Mann, author of the original novel, told Jannings during production that 'the success of this film will be found in the naked thighs of Miss Dietrich!'

'She makes reason totter on her throne' wrote the critic James Agate. Marlene Dietrich, who for so many years defied time, has also denied history. For more than two decades she included in her remarkable stage act some fragments of purely mythical autobiography that obliterated all that she had achieved before Josef von Sternberg made her an international star with *Der Blaue Engel*.

Dietrich has claimed that she was an unknown drama student when Sternberg 'discovered' her. She was, in fact, a veteran of 7 years and 17 films, not counting walk-on parts that date from as early as 1919.

Never the most modest of men, even Sternberg grew irritated with her insistence that he was her 'Svengali':

'She has never ceased to proclaim that I taught her everything. Among the many things I did not teach her was to be garrulous about me . . . I did not endow her with a personality that was not her own; one sees what one wants to see, and I gave her nothing that she did not already have. What I did was to dramatize her attributes and make them visible for all to see; though, as there were perhaps too many, I concealed some.'

The new angel

Maria Magdalene Dietrich was born in 1901, the daughter of an officer in the Royal Prussian Police. Abandoning a musical training in favour of the stage, she telescoped her names into 'Marlene' and in January 1922 had her first break with a small part in *Der Grosse Bariton* (The Great Baritone).

Her first credited film role is as a maid-servant, helping her mistress to escape, in the comic costume romance *So Sind die Männer* (1922, Men Are Like This). In Joe May's

Right: the myth takes shape in the silent Three Loves.

Tragödie der Liebe (1923, *Tragedy of Love*), a rambling four-part murder serial starring Emil Jannings, she plays the girlfriend of a lawyer.

She moved into supporting roles in films which included *Manon Lescaut* (1926), and *Cafe Electric* (1927), and was leading lady to the 'adventure king' Harry Piel in *Sein Grösster Bluff* (1927, His Greatest Bluff). Alexander Korda cast her as a coquette, enraged by the shopgirl heroine who borrows her gown in *Eine Dubarry von Heute* (1926, A Modern Dubarry). in *Ich Küsse Ihre Hand, Madame* (1929, *I Kiss Your Hand, Madame*) she has an unrewarding lead part in an operetta tale of thwarted love and mistaken identity. In Maurice Tourneur's *Das Schiff der Verlorenen Menschen* (1929, The Ship of Lost Souls), she is again in the lead, playing an aeronaut pursued by the woman-hungry crew of the ship that rescues her from a crash.

Fatal attractions

Die Frau, nach der Man Sich Sehnt (1929, *Three Loves*), directed by Kurt Bernhardt, showed a clear understanding of Dietrich's *femme fatale* quality and strange sexual aura.

She bewitches a young man on his honeymoon – travelling on the same train – and begs him to rescue her from her sinister companion, later revealed to be her lover. He abandons his bride to pursue this lovely creature, but she seems unable, or unwilling, to break from Karoff, her jealous lover who, it seems, has murdered her husband with her knowledge. She eventually dies at Karoff's hands. The decorative manner of this film remarkably anticipates the visual style of Sternberg: in a party scene, balloons and streamers fill the air to confuse and torment the characters; lighting is used to model the star's face; and in one memorable shot a shaft of light from an opening door gradually creeps up Dietrich's silk-clad legs, with startlingly sensuous effect.

It is apparent that somebody already recognized the mythical possibilities of Dietrich. The tempting conclusion is that it was the star herself, for it was she who approached the writers Walter Wassermann and Walter Schlee to give her a 'similar script' for her next film. They obliged with *Gefahren der Brautzeit* (1929, Dangers of the Engagement), in which a baron meets an unknown beauty (Dietrich) on

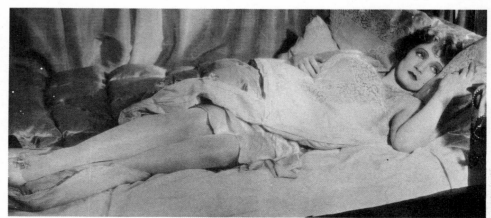

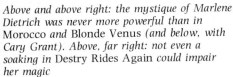

Above and above right: the mystique of Marlene Dietrich was never more powerful than in Morocco *and* Blonde Venus *(and below, with Cary Grant). Above, far right: not even a soaking in* Destry Rides Again *could impair her magic*

a train; the first glimpse of her, framed in a frosted carriage window, might well be from a Sternberg film. The train breaks down and the couple spend a night of love in a hotel. The next morning the lady has disappeared. Arriving at his destination the Baron meets his best friend, who introduces his fiancée – the unknown beauty. She later comes to the Baron's room to tell him their meeting must be forgotten; but they are surprised by her betrothed who shoots his friend in a fit of jealousy. The Baron pretends the injury is nothing and succeeds in reconciling the couple; he then dies alone, using his last strength to feign suicide. The film is almost a carbon copy of its predecessor, with the significant difference that here it is the man, not the *femme fatale*, who dies.

And along came Jo
Then Josef von Sternberg entered her life. According to him, he chose Dietrich for the part of Lola-Lola after seeing her on stage in *Zwei Krawatten* (Two Neckties). Only later did he see her screen-work which he described as: '. . . an ordeal. If I had first seen her films . . . my reaction would have been the same as everyone else's. In them she was an awkward, unattractive woman, left to her own devices, and presented in an embarrassing exhibition of drivel.'

This is patently untrue, though perhaps Sternberg saw the wrong films. In *Die Frau, nach der Man Sich Sehnt* and *Gefahren der Brautzeit* the form of the mythical Marlene is evident, though still rough-hewn. Sternberg's role was to perfect it, and provide a wonderful visual framework for the image: 'What I did was to dramatize her attributes and make them visible for all to see'.

This extraordinary man was born Jonas Sternberg in Vienna in 1894. His early life seems to have been a struggle for survival and self-education, which permanently marked a sensitive but defiantly arrogant personality.

Emigrating to the United States as a child, he found his way into the cinema, worked his way up in various technical jobs, and in 1925 directed a low-budget, independently produced feature, *The Salvation Hunters*. It brought him work in Hollywood on successful silents like the gangster story, *Underworld* (1927), and *The Last Command* (1928), which earned Emil Jannings the first Best Actor Oscar.

As a result Jannings, having now returned to Germany, requested Sternberg as the director of his first all-talkie film – *Der Blaue Engel* (*The Blue Angel*). The film was a triumph and so was its leading lady – Dietrich.

The road to Morocco
Summoned by Paramount, she departed immediately after the film's premiere. She was preceded by Sternberg, who had persuaded the studio to sign her and was the obvious choice to direct her first American film.

Again Dietrich seems to have taken the initiative in selecting her vehicle. She is said to have given Sternberg a copy of the novel *Amy Jolly* to read on the boat. Later she cabled him that it was, after all, 'weak lemonade' but Sternberg proceeded to make *Morocco* (1930) from it. The story centres on a woman (Dietrich plays another cabaret artist) whose feelings are divided between loyalty to a wealthy socialite (Adolphe Menjou) and passion for a legionnaire (Gary Cooper) whom she eventually follows into the desert. Even today the sexual suggestions and ambivalences in Marlene's cabaret act can still raise eyebrows. In any event, *Morocco* consolidated the legend and securely launched her American career.

Paramount partners
In the next five years Dietrich and Sternberg worked together on five more films that, ultimately, were to elevate her into a screen goddess. In *Dishonored* (1931) she is a beautiful spy in the Mata Hari mould, dying with *sangfroid* in front of the firing squad. In *Shanghai Express* (1932) she is spellbindingly erotic as Shanghai Lily, the woman with a past, sacrificing herself to a Chinese rebel to save the man she loves. This is perhaps Sternberg's most perfect film; visual spectacle and narrative are totally integrated. In *Blonde Venus* (1932) she

is a woman who turns singer (and perhaps worse) to pay for the operations needed to save her husband's life. Perhaps the most startling sequence of *Blonde Venus* is the 'Hot Voodoo' number in the nightclub with its chorus of spear-carrying girls. In the midst of them Dietrich emerges, like a butterfly out of a chrysalis, from a huge and hairy gorilla suit, which she proceeds to remove before singing the song. In *The Scarlet Empress* (1934), a witty interpretation of history, she is a sensuous Catherine the Great. In *The Devil Is a Woman* (1935) she becomes a Spanish siren who enslaves a young political refugee and an older grandee. Here Sternberg's ability to decorate the *femme fatale* myth reached a peak, but the film's commercial failure (the Spanish government demanded its withdrawal) was the excuse for Paramount, alarmed by his extravagance and dogged independence, to end his contract. In any case, he had announced during filming that it would benefit neither Dietrich nor himself to stay together.

The parting of the ways

'I didn't leave Sternberg. *He* left *me*!' Dietrich told the *Sunday Times* nearly 30 years later. 'That's very important. In my life, he was the man I wanted to please most. He decided not to work with me any more and I was very unhappy about that.'

Dietrich's dependence and attachment to Sternberg were intense. Sternberg's wife had earlier sued her for alienation of affection and libel. Dietrich won the case but it sparked off a great deal of controversy and speculation about the exact nature of the union between the director and his protégée, and may have been a major cause of their separation.

Only once between *Der Blaue Engel* and *The Devil Is a Woman* had Dietrich worked under another director – Rouben Mamoulian in *Song of Songs* (1933). It was apparently an uneasy collaboration for director and star. Dietrich is said to have been in the habit of murmuring into the microphone before a take 'Where are you, Jo?' In later years she herself elaborated this story; her actual words, she told director Peter Bogdanovich (*Esquire*, January 1973) were 'Oh Jo – why hast thou forsaken me?'

For both director and star, the cycle of pictures they made together represented the summit of their achievement in the cinema. Sternberg had proved himself one of Hollywood's supreme artists, with Dietrich at the centre of the decadent, dreamlike world created by his lush, exotic style. He worked on only 9 more features in the remaining 18 years of his career, and of these, Korda's *I, Claudius* (1937) was abandoned and 3 were reworked by other directors. Only *The Shanghai Gesture* (1941) and *The Saga of Anatahan* (1953) can stand alongside the great Sternberg pictures of the Thirties.

Dietrich's career also suffered a decline. She made the kitschy *The Garden of Allah* (1936) with Richard Boleslavsky; a couple of frothy comedies, Frank Borzage's *Desire* (1936) and Ernst Lubitsch's *Angel* (1937); and in Britain, Jacques Feyder's beautiful but dull *Knight Without Armour* (1937). By this time she was ungallantly labelled 'box-office poison' and ranked at number 126 in the list of money-making stars. Shortly afterwards Paramount announced: 'Marlene Dietrich will be permitted to work elsewhere'.

Dietrich rides again

Her career revived dramatically in 1939 with George Marshall's tongue-in-cheek Western, *Destry Rides Again*, in which she plays Frenchy, a saloon singer in love with the mild-mannered sheriff (James Stewart). None of the many films that followed framed and deified her as carefully as the Sternberg pictures had done; but by this time it hardly seemed to matter. The myth was already complete, unchangeable and impregnable, and – whatever Sternberg may have contributed – it was clear that its conservation was mostly due to Dietrich herself.

We have the evidence of nearly everybody who worked with her that nothing she did was accidental or unconscious. Lee Garmes, Sternberg's cameraman, said, 'She had a great mechanical mind and knew the camera. She would always stop in the exact position that was right for her . . .' Harry Stradling, who filmed *The Garden of Allah*, confirmed:

'While each shot was being lined up she had a full-length mirror set up beside the camera and was able to see just how she would look on the screen. If she thought the light on her arms was too strong, or her shoulders were catching too much from a certain arc, she never hesitated to say so; and she was always right.'

Perhaps the surest proof of her great professionalism lay in the dramatic roles she played in her last pictures: the wife giving treacherous evidence in Billy Wilder's *Witness for the Prosecution* (1957); the tough madame in Orson Welles's *Touch of Evil* (1958); and the widow of a Nazi general in Stanley Kramer's *Judgement at Nuremberg* (1961). To be a star and a myth, she revealed, did not preclude intelligent and concentrated dramatic interpretation. Then in 1979, after a 16-year absence, she returned to the screen, playing another madame in David Hemmings's *Just A Gigolo*. Her career in motion pictures now spans over 60 years.

The eternal superstar

Yet the masterpiece of the myth was perhaps the Dietrich who emerged as a solo concert performer during and after World War II.

In 1953 she began the series of tours that were to take her around the world. Dietrich never disappointed her audiences. And every night the myth was brought to life on stage. In private she could be a loving mother and wife (Dietrich married Rudolf Sieber, one of Joe May's production assistants, in 1924), an industrious housekeeper, a practical and willing nurse, a determined trouper and a sensible traveller. On stage, however, the glamour of that solitary figure, sheathed in sequins and furs, never flickered; it defied all the inroads of time. And her performance was not just a magnificent illusion. When she sang 'Where Have All the Flowers Gone' and 'Lili Marlene', or touched the past with 'Falling in Love Again', she became a tragic actress – as well as a mythical figure encompassing a lifetime of all our history.   DAVID ROBINSON

Quotations from: Fun in a Chinese Laundry *by Josef von Sternberg;* Marlene Dietrich *by Sheridan Morley; All My Yesterdays *by Edward G. Robinson.*

Filmography

1922 So Sind die Männer/Napoleons Kleiner Brüder/Der Kleine Napoleon. '23 Tragödie der Liebe (USA/GB: Tragedy of Love); Der Mensch am Wege. '24 Der Sprung ins Leben/Die Roman eine Zirkuskindes. '25 Die Freudlose Gasse (USA: Streets of Sorrow, reissued with post-synchronized sound in 1937 as The Street of Sorrow; GB: The Joyless Street). '26 Manon Lescaut; Eine Dubarry von Heute; Kopf Hoch, Charly!; Madame Wünscht Keine Kinder; Der Juxbaron. '27 Sein Grösster Bluff/Er Oder Dich; Cafe Electric/Wenn ein Weib den Weg Verliert (A: Die Liebesbörse). '28 Prinzessin Olala; Die Glückliche Mutter (short: edited version of home movies made by her husband in mid-1920s, reputedly shown publicly). '29 Ich Küsse Ihre Hand, Madame (USA: I Kiss Your Hand, Madame); Die Frau, nach der Man Sich Sehnt (USA/GB: Three Loves); Das Schiff der Verlorenen Menschen; Gefahren der Brautzeit/Liebesnächte. '30 Der Blaue Engel (English-language version: The Blue Angel, USA/GB, 1931). *All remaining films USA unless specified:* '30 Morocco. '31 Dishonored. '32 Shanghai Express; Blonde Venus. '33 The Song of Songs. '34 The Scarlet Empress. '35 The Devil Is a Woman. '36 Desire; I Loved a Soldier (unfinished; refilmed without her as Hotel Imperial in 1939); The Garden of Allah. '37 Knight Without Armour (GB); Angel. '39 Destry Rides Again. '40 Seven Sinners; The Flame of New Orleans; Manpower. '42 The Lady Is Willing; The Spoilers; Pittsburgh. '43 Stage Door Canteen (publicity sketch not used in actual film). '44 Follow the Boys (guest); Kismet. '46 Martin Roumagnac (FR) (USA: The Room Upstairs). '47 Golden Earrings. '48 A Foreign Affair. '49 Jigsaw (guest); Stage Fright (GB). '51 No Highway (GB) (USA: No Highway in the Sky). '52 Rancho Notorious. '56 Around the World in 80 Days (guest); The Monte Carlo Story. '57 Witness for the Prosecution. '58 Touch of Evil (guest). '61 Judgement at Nuremberg. '62 The Black Fox (narr. only). '63 Paris When It Sizzles (guest). '79 Schöner Gigolo – Armer Gigolo (GER) (GB: Just a Gigolo).

Below: Dietrich as the madame in Just a Gigolo; *half a century after* The Blue Angel *and the allure of Lola-Lola lingers on*

File on Fonda

'I want to be responsible, positive, constructive. And I want to be the best actress I can be. I am a political animal, I am a woman who is personally engaged, and I am an actress. It has taken me some time to reconcile the two positions.'
Jane Fonda

It is hardly a new phenomenon for the children of famous show-business personalities to follow them into careers in the entertainment world. However, as Liza Minnelli once commented:

'Of course your parents' names open doors, but at 8.30 when the curtain goes up, it's you out there, not them. Without something of your own, those same doors can shut fast.'

The truth of that can be seen in the fact that Henry Fonda's name opened doors for both of his children, but while daughter Jane became an important international star with a reputation as a serious actress, her brother Peter's career, after an auspicious beginning, simply petered out.

Born in 1937 (her mother was Frances Brokaw), Jane went with her father to the East Coast when, in 1948, he went to New York to star in the Broadway production of *Mister Roberts*. She lived with her grandmother in nearby Connecticut, and then studied at Vassar, where she did a little acting in University productions. In the early Fifties her father cast her in his summer stock productions of the plays *The Country Girl* and *The Male Animal*. She was so dissatisfied with her own performances that she gave up acting to study

painting (in Paris) and piano (in New York). Feeling she was even less gifted at those two disciplines, she returned to enrol at Lee Strasberg's Actors Studio, supporting herself by modelling. Then the Fonda name began to open doors.

Joshua Logan – an old friend of her father – cast her in the college comedy *Tall Story* (1960) as a newly married cheer-leader, and in the ill-fated Broadway show *There Was a Little Girl*.

The reviews of both were negative, and her personal notices were, at best, mixed. After another Broadway failure – *The Fun Couple* – she returned to movies. Critical opinion remained unsure as she moved through a mostly mediocre series of films, playing a prostitute in *Walk on the Wild Side*, a frigid wife in *The Chapman Report*, a naive bride in *Period of Adjustment* (all 1962), and an adultress in *In the Cool of the Day* (1963). While the satirical magazine *Harvard Lampoon* named her 'the year's worst actress', both critics and audiences were beginning to notice that she had

Top: the two faces of baby Jane – as space-age seductress Barbarella *with David Hemmings (left), and with husband-to-be Tom Hayden (right) on a troublesome visit to Britain in 1972 to promote their anti-Vietnam War campaign. Below: In the Cool of the Day Murray Logan (Peter Finch) has an affair with a colleague's wife (Fonda)*

something; that magnetic quality which makes an actress watchable, no matter how awful the vehicle. She was also obviously sincere, intelligent, and attempting to make something worthwhile out of even the trashiest dialogue and situations. The fact that she was sexy and oddly beautiful kept her career going in spite of the less than magnificent box-office results.

It is impossible to guess what might have happened to that career – and her life – had she then not been called to France to appear in René Clément's *Les Félins* (1964, *The Love Cage*), in which (not surprisingly) her cool sexuality failed to strike sparks from Alain Delon's own glacial eroticism. But her temporary role as an international sex symbol – 'the American Bardot' – had begun. Immediately after the Clément film, she went to work in Roger Vadim's *La Ronde* (1964, *Circle of Love*). When asked later why she married her lover – the director who 'created' Bardot and was known for his elegant sex films – she said it was because he was charming, dashing, romantic and represented a kind of world that was very foreign to her.

Over the next five years, she returned to the United States to work but she lived in France. Vadim and Fonda had a daughter (Vanessa) and made four films together, in all of which she moved through titillating situations in various stages of undress. The most commercially successful of them was *Barbarella* (1968), based on a comic strip, and emphasizing even more than usual Vadim's cinematic conception of woman as sexual object and plaything. That particular image was, in reality, one which Fonda herself was less and less comfortable with.

Although she has since turned her back on the work done before *They Shoot Horses, Don't They?* (1969) – referring to that part of her output as 'when I wasn't very good' – she has never said even the least negative thing about ex-husband Vadim, with whom she has remained friendly. She now sees her experience in France as valuable: in 1968 France exploded politically, and more than a few people were politicized for the first time in their lives. Jane Fonda was one of them.

Above: Dove Linkhorn (Laurence Harvey) meets lost love Kitty Twist (Fonda) working in a brothel in Walk on the Wild Side. *Left: as a prostitute again in* Klute. *Below left: Jane at home with father Henry, husband Vadim and daughter Vanessa. Below:* They Shoot Horses, Don't They? *is a painful portrayal of the dance marathons of the Depression; Gloria (Fonda) and Robert (Michael Sarrazin) battle on*

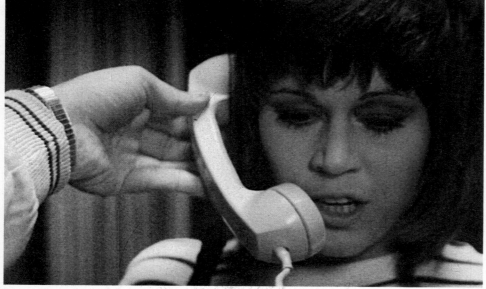

By 1970 she was often called Hanoi Jane, and was as well known for her political activities as for her screen performances. She explained that she came from a bourgeois, liberal background – her father was a Roosevelt and Stevenson Democrat – and she, like her family, had donated money to various liberal causes and had signed petitions without actually engaging in politics on a personal level. It was the atrocities and misleading reports concerning Vietnam that led her to become interested – and active – in various causes, including the rights of American Indians and blacks and, most importantly, ending the war in Vietnam.

Whereas she won well-deserved awards for her performance as the threatened prostitute in *Klute* (1971), it was about the same time that the press and government crucified her as a 'traitor' and worse. She became active in the Free The Army movement, touring American Army bases with a revue in an attempt to get soldiers to refuse to fight in Vietnam. Neither of the two films which resulted from those tours – *F.T.A.* (1972) and *Steelyard Blues* (1973) – received wide distribution. She also returned to France briefly to appear in Jean-Luc Godard's *Tout Va Bien* (1972, All Goes Well), a forthrightly political film concerning, among other things, a strike in a factory. Fonda was not entirely pleased with either the film or with Godard as a director – a compliment he returned in the short *A Letter to Jane, or Investigation About a Still* (1973), which features a still photograph of her. This was an analysis of what he saw as Fonda's superficial

Left: Fonda continued her anti-war protest on film with Donald Sutherland in Steelyard Blues. *Below left: in* Coming Home, *Jon Voight plays a crippled veteran. Below: with James Caan in* Comes a Horseman (1978)

and 'radical chic' approach to the war and revolution.

Since then, Fonda admits that her one error during the period of her first politicization and the anti-war movement was that she was shrill – preaching rather than talking to audiences – and that there was the chance that she alienated many who then refused to listen to her. She has noted that people now tell her she has become more human, although she has not become any less political. She works actively with her politician husband, Tom Hayden, for the political organization they founded – the California Campaign for Economic Democracy. At least half of her films now have something of a political message: the war and returning Vietnam veterans in *Coming Home* (1978), the dangers of nuclear power plants in *The China Syndrome* (1979), the lives of 'repression' lived by office secretaries in *9 to 5* (1980). Yet, there is, now, a difference:

'I chose to do *Fun With Dick and Jane* (1977)

No longer the sexy nymphet, Jane Fonda's screen image is now one of social and political concern – TV reporter in The China Syndrome *(top) or militant secretary with Dolly Parton and Lily Tomlin in* 9 to 5 *(above)*

because I thought the time had come to do a comedy, a film which would be commercial, a film in which I was pretty. It showed I was a good actress and that I was commercial. I think that *The China Syndrome* had a social and commercial impact that was very strong. It is an example of a fusion of two kinds of film. We wanted to have a film which said something we wanted to say, but we wanted to attract the widest possible audience to say it to. It functions as a suspense film, but it is also about something important in the daily lives of those who see it. Let's not exaggerate, of course. No film can support a mass movement. Films can have a certain effect, but they represent only a small step in a certain direction. I think I now

understand how to say things and still have a large number of people listen. In the new film we wanted to say something about the condition of secretaries, but *9 to 5* is first of all a very funny comedy.'

At a time when she has won all the acting awards available, when she is often called the most interesting actress of her generation (and not just by her father), she still claims to be frightened with each new role:

'I always think another actress would be better in the role. When I played Bree in *Klute*, I went to bars where prostitutes hung out to prepare the role. Nobody made even a single proposition to me and I went back terrified to Alan Pakula and told him I was obviously wrong for the role. Still, that's getting better and better, because I am beginning to know what I am capable of.' DAVID OVERBEY

Quotations are taken from an interview by Henri Béhar, part of which was published in the May 1979 issue of Premiere.

Filmography
1960 Tall Story. **'62** Walk on the Wild Side; The Chapman Report; Period of Adjustment. **'63** In the Cool of the Day; Jane (doc) (appearance as herself only); Sunday in New York. **'64** Les Félins (FR) (USA: The Joy House; GB: The Love Cage); La Ronde (FR-IT) (USA: Circle of Love). **'65** Cat Ballou. **'66** The Chase; La Curée (FR-IT) (USA/GB: The Game Is Over); Any Wednesday (GB: Bachelor Girl Apartment). **'67** Hurry Sundown; Barefoot in the Park. **'68** Histoires Extraordinaires *ep* Metzengerstein only (FR-IT) (USA: Spirits of the Dead; GB: Tales of Mystery); Barbarella (FR-IT). **'69** They Shoot Horses, Don't They? **'71** Klute. **'72** Tout Va Bien; F.T.A. (+co-prod;+co-sc). **'73** Steelyard Blues (re-released in USA as: Final Crash); A Doll's House (GB-FR). **'74** Jane Fonda on Vietnam (doc. short) (NOR) (appearance as herself only); Vietnam Journey: Introduction to the Enemy (doc) (+co-dir;+appearance as herself). **'76** The Blue Bird (USA-USSR). **'77** Fun With Dick and Jane; Julia. **'78** Coming Home; Comes a Horseman; California Suite. **'79** The China Syndrome; The Electric Horseman. **'80** 9 to 5; No Nukes (appearance as self only). **'81** On Golden Pond.

Joan Fontaine

Sweet little tough girl

Joan Fontaine began her starring career as Hollywood's idea of a pure English rose; when it turned out that this rose had thorns, things went considerably less well. She was, in fact, the daughter of British parents, born in Japan in 1917, a year later than her sister Olivia de Havilland. Her parents separated in 1921 and she went with her mother and sister to California where she was brought up. She began acting in amateur and semi-professional productions with a local theatre group when still in her teens, spurred on no doubt by the early success of her sister; their rivalry later provided the fan magazines with a fertile topic for many years. Her first film role was in *No More Ladies* (1935), with Joan Crawford and Robert Montgomery. But her appearance made no impression, and neither did an equally unimportant role in *Quality Street* (1937) as a pale English miss. However, she was signed to an RKO contract and actually starred in a couple of films, most notably opposite Fred Astaire (taking a short break from Ginger) in *A Damsel in Distress* (1937). Increasingly she found herself in minor films until she was dropped by RKO, picked up briefly by MGM to play a timid girl in *The Women* (1939), and again dropped.

The most noticeable quality of her earliest performances seems to be sheer, blind panic. If it could be harnessed and properly used, she promised to be remarkable. The realization of this came with *Rebecca* (1940), in which, after a much-publicized search for the right actress (like the one mounted for Scarlett O'Hara), David O. Selznick cast her as the shrinking second wife (with no name) of Rebecca's widower in Hitchcock's adaptation of Daphne du Maurier's best-selling novel. Hitchcock allegedly treated her throughout the shooting as though wrapped in cotton wool. She gave one of those performances in which the player and the part are indistinguishable, was nominated for an Oscar, and became at once a star. Off screen, Joan Fontaine immediately began to

show her thorns: she refused to do what Selznick wanted her to until she felt the part was suitable. In the end she followed up *Rebecca* with another, similar role of a menaced wife in Hitchcock's *Suspicion* (1941), and this time she got her Oscar.

It was, really, the high-point of her career, though she remained a top-billed, highly paid star for many years afterwards. She was still English and menaced in *Jane Eyre* in 1943, and in *Frenchman's Creek* (1944), another adaptation from du Maurier, she managed to handle a pirate's affections with fair aplomb,

Above left: Joan Fontaine as a New York wife facing hard times in From This Day Forward. *Above: in* Suspicion. *Right: in her other film for Hitchcock. Below: as a schoolteacher in her last picture,* The Witches

and looked gorgeous in Technicolor. From time to time she was permitted to play Americans – most touchingly coping with the problems of life in peacetime for a working-class New York couple in *From This Day Forward* (1946). She played an Austrian countess in love with a record-player salesman (Bing Crosby) in Billy Wilder's *The Emperor Waltz* (1948) and an Austrian waif in love with a musician (Louis Jourdan) in Max Ophuls' *Letter From an Unknown Woman* (1948), perhaps her best performance.

From then on she began to get tougher roles. She battled with alcoholism in *Something to Live For* (1952), hopped saucily in and out of bed in *Decameron Nights* (1952), coped with her husband's bigamy in *The Bigamist* (1953), and fought for her lover whom she believed had unjustly been convicted of murder in the last and least of Fritz Lang's American films, *Beyond a Reasonable Doubt* (1956). Smallish though still starring roles in big productions like *Island in the Sun* (1957) and *Tender Is the Night* (1962) followed. But then she virtually retired from the screen except for the British-made horror film *The Witches* (1966).

The quality that made Joan Fontaine a big star was small but genuine: the ability to project fear and vulnerability in such a way that everyone in the audience wanted to protect her. Once she began to seem tough or brittle she was effective enough, but routine. In *Rebecca* and *Letter From an Unknown Woman*, however, she could hardly have been bettered.

JOHN RUSSELL TAYLOR

Filmography

As Joan Burfield: **1935** No More Ladies. *As Joan Fontaine:* **'37** Quality Street; The Man Who Found Himself; You Can't Beat Love; Music for Madame; A Damsel in Distress; A Million to One. **'38** Maid's Night Out; Blond Cheat; Sky Giant; The Duke of West Point. **'39** Gunga Din; Man of Conquest; The Women. **'40** Rebecca. **'41** Suspicion. **'42** This Above All. **'43** The Constant Nymph; Jane Eyre. **'44** Frenchman's Creek. **'45** The Affairs of Susan. **'46** From This Day Forward. **'47** Ivy. **'48** Letter From an Unknown Woman; The Emperor Waltz; Kiss the Blood Off My Hands (GB: Blood on My Hands); You Gotta Stay Happy. **'50** Born to Be Bad; September Affair. **'51** Darling, How Could You! (GB: Rendezvous). **'52** Something to Live For; Othello (guest, uncredited); Ivanhoe (GB); Decameron Nights (GB). **'53** Flight to Tangier; The Bigamist; Casanova's Big Night. **'56** Serenade; Beyond a Reasonable Doubt. **'57** The Ghost and Mrs Muir (short); Island in the Sun; Until They Sail. **'58** A Certain Smile. **'61** Voyage to the Bottom of the Sea. **'62** Tender Is the Night. **'66** The Witches (GB) (USA: The Devil's Own).

GARBO

Of all the silent stars in the Hollywood galaxy, Garbo's was the voice that excited most speculation. Millions of her adoring fans around the world anxiously awaited the screen goddess's first talking film, hoping for a true insight into the secrets of her elusive personality

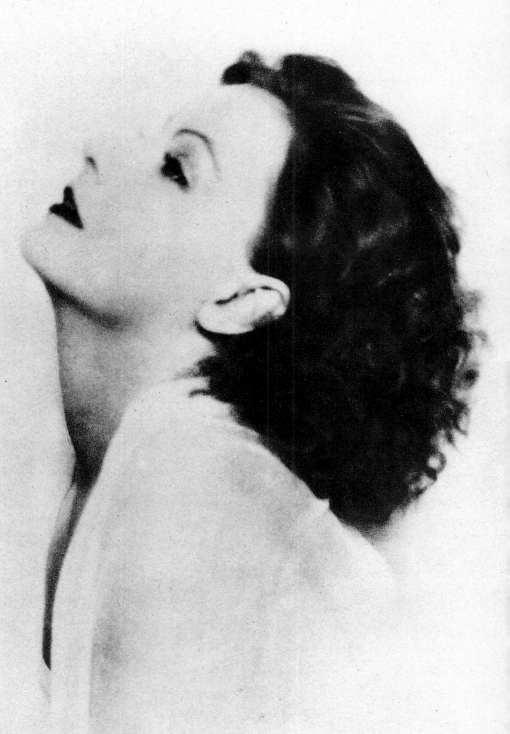

Greta Garbo gave maturity and passion to the Hollywood heroine. Instead of being petite and childlike, everything about her was large – her hands, her mouth, her feet. She filled the screen with a powerful physical presence. She portrayed love as a glorious rapture, freely given, not an unwilling submission granted a suitor with the reluctance of a miser parting with small change. Where others simpered pretty endearments or coyly fluttered their eyelashes, Garbo's entire body expressed love with a vibrant intensity that came as a revelation to American audiences.

Greta Garbo was born Greta Gustafsson, the youngest of three children, in Stockholm, on September 18, 1905. Her father's death, when she was 14, forced her to seek work in a department store, where she modelled fashion for magazines and short advertising films. These led to her being cast in a two-reel comedy *Luffar-Petter* (1922, *Peter the Tramp*), made by director Erik Petschler. She obviously enjoyed the experience for she then applied to, and was accepted by, Stockholm's famous Royal School of Dramatic Art.

She soon came to the attention of Mauritz Stiller, one of Sweden's two leading film directors, who cast her in a supporting but pivotal rolé, that of Countess Elizabeth, in *Gösta Berlings Saga* (1924, *The Atonement of Gösta Berling*). He also changed her name to the shorter and more evocative Garbo – a Spanish word meaning 'graceful'.

Their next film was to have been shot in Istanbul, but the backing company, Trianon, went bankrupt before filming began, and Garbo travelled instead to Berlin to appear in G.W. Pabst's *Die Freudlose Gasse* (1925, *The Joyless Street*), opposite the Danish star Asta Nielsen. As both the Stiller and the Pabst films were major works by major film-makers, and her roles in them were significant, her career was now securely launched. However, she was destined to be more than a European celebrity. Louis B. Mayer, vice-president and general manager of MGM (Metro-Goldwyn-Mayer), was talent hunting while on holiday with his family in Europe, and signed up both her and Stiller for Hollywood.

I never said, 'I want to be alone,' I only said, 'I want to be let alone.' There is all the difference. Greta Garbo

---

She arrived in Los Angeles in the late autumn of 1925 with Mauritz Stiller, her discoverer, director and mentor. It is generally said that her presence was part of a package deal: to get Stiller, Mayer also had to take the great man's protégée. But biographies of Mayer suggest that he signed her, quite independently of any other deal, to a standard seven-year contract at a starting salary of

$400 per week for the first year, rising to $600 per week in her second year.

Having found her, Hollywood at first appeared unsure of how to handle her. She was not eager to throw herself into the activities that were standard procedure for building a starlet – publicity photos with performing seals, tame lions and visiting sportsmen; press interviews, parties and other social functions – and indeed, once her English became good enough for her to understand what was being asked of her, she firmly refused to 'perform'.

> *I was the one who insisted on closed sets for her. No visitors, and so on, no one present except the director and the crew, and no executives. I was trying to help her, especially because it took her a time to speak English, and she was so shy, so shy . . .*
> *William Daniels*

But although MGM was still working out what to do with Garbo, her public was already waiting. This audience, who had worshipped the romantic heroines of the early silent screen, now wanted something new. The Twenties, after all, were the time of Prohibition, bobbed hair and the New Morality. The war too had changed people's attitudes. The men who had fought in Europe had come home with new ideas. They still wanted to see their fantasies on the screen but their fantasies had changed, and the old stars did not fulfil them any longer.

MGM finally cast Garbo as a Spanish peasant girl in *The Torrent* (1926), a romantic melodrama starring Ricardo Cortez. The announcement that it was to be directed by Monta Bell came as a blow to both Garbo and Stiller. William Daniels was the cameraman on *The Torrent*. It was the start of a long relationship – he was to make 19 films with Garbo. In

Hollywood Cameramen, by Charles Higham, he recalled:

'My memory of my first meeting with her is very clear . . . They asked me to come in one Sunday morning and do some tests of a Swedish girl. She had just arrived . . . There she was, in the midst of a strange people and a strange language, and it must have been a horrifying experience for her . . . We lit very much to find [an actress's] best features and accent those features strongly. Especially eyes. And Garbo had magnificent eyes . . .'

The success of *The Torrent* showed that public and critics alike were in no doubt about Garbo's qualities. *Motion Picture* said: 'Making her debut in the film, she registers a complete success. She is not so much an actress as she is endowed with individuality and magnetism.'

Her range of mood and expression was also immediately apparent in this first film as the *New York Herald Tribune* observed: 'She seems an excellent and attractive actress with a surprising propensity for looking like Carol Dempster, Norma Talmadge, ZaSu Pitts, and Gloria Swanson in turn. That does not mean she lacks a manner of her own, however.'

Reactions to her next film, *The Temptress* (1926), with co-star Antonio Moreno, were just as warm. The *Life* critic announced that

Above: Greta Gustafsson (left) in her first film role in Peter the Tramp. *Below: Mauritz Stiller, her friend and mentor, directs Garbo and co-star Antonio Moreno in* The Temptress. *Sadly MGM disliked Stiller's approach and took him off the film*

Miss Garbo had knocked him for a loop, and the *New York Times* noticed that 'with a minimum of gestures and an unusual restraint in her expressions, she makes every scene in which she appears a telling one. The *New York Herald Tribune* felt that 'she is a magnetic woman and a finished actress. In fact, she leaves nothing to be desired. Such a profile, such grace, and most of all, such eyelashes . . . not a conventional beauty, yet she makes all the other beauties seem a little obvious.'

By being worshipped by the entire world, she gives you the feeling that if your imagination has to sin, it can at least congratulate itself on its impeccable taste.
Alistair Cooke

The public thought so too, copying her natural makeup, loose hair styles and casual clothes. They loved her remoteness, her diffidence, the looks she cast, the emancipated way she acted and reacted, and the halting, hesitant, half-awkward, coltish way she moved. It was not that she rebelled against the established conventions, but that she seemed so at home outside them. She came across on the screen as an erotic, mysterious being who coolly dominated situations, yet became sublimely feminine and tender in solitude.

Filming of *The Temptress* started under the direction of Mauritz Stiller, but shortly after shooting began he was replaced by Fred Niblo. It appears that Stiller's working methods were not those of the studio. He did not understand its insistence on strict shooting schedules and budgets. He left MGM and went to Paramount where he made three films during the following year. He then returned to Sweden but died soon afterwards.

While the sophisticated, world-famous Stiller was buckling in the face of studio demands, the shy, 21-year-old Garbo was

Left: Garbo and John Gilbert were a smash hit in Flesh and the Devil, *especially when rumours spread of their real-life romance*

calmly incurring the studio's wrath rather than play another temptress in *Flesh and the Devil* (1927). She received telegrams and letters ordering her to report for costume fittings – first from the director of publicity and then from studio production head Irving Thalberg. Finally Louis B. Mayer himself, in a letter that alternated between commanding and wheedling, ordered her to report for work, telling her how difficult it was to find suitable roles for her. It is interesting to note that all these letters stressed that failure to observe these orders should not be interpreted as a termination of her contract with the studio. Mayer would cut off her salary but would not risk losing her to a competitor.

Garbo finally gave in, but it was to be the only battle with the studio that she lost. In future, she would be able to sit out such storms or else threaten to quit with the famous words, 'I t'ink I go home'.

In this case it was fortunate that Garbo had to accept her role in *Flesh and the Devil* as the film was crucial in making her a top star. It was skilfully directed by Clarence Brown who became her favourite director, guiding her through six more films. In an interview for *Focus on Film* he recalled:

'I made six pictures with her. Nobody else could make over two. I had a way with Garbo that didn't embarrass her. Garbo is a very sensitive person, and, in those days directors used to yell from behind the camera. I never gave her directions in front of anyone else.'

Garbo is marvellous, the most alluring creature you have seen. Capricious as the devil, whimsical . . . and fascinating.
John Gilbert

In her third American film she was teamed with two male stars – John Gilbert and Lars Hanson. Gilbert was the nation's romantic idol; for the first and only time she had to settle for second billing.

The public were about to get something more than three of their favourite stars in a triangular tale of love and tragedy – they were to witness a real love story. It seems Gilbert had fallen madly in love with Garbo and she with him. 'In their scenes together', said Clarence Brown 'it was working with raw material. They were in that blissful state of love which is so like a rosy cloud that they imagined themselves hidden behind it.' They co-starred in only four films; three came at the height of their affair – *Flesh and the Devil* and *Love* (both 1927), and *A Woman of Affairs* (1928).

After the romance ended, Garbo went on to other heights, while Gilbert's popularity started to wane. However in 1933, when Gilbert had severe problems in both his personal life and his career, Garbo insisted on him being her co-star in *Queen Christina*, although she had already approved the younger and more suitable Laurence Olivier. That she should have had this request granted says much about the power of her position at MGM, for all Hollywood knew that Mayer hated Gilbert, and Garbo's decision was clearly offensive to him.

Her position at the studio was already

Garbo's enigmatic image made her an ideal spy, both in Mata Hari *(above) and in* The Mysterious Lady *(below)*

clearly established in 1927 when, after *Flesh and the Devil*, she refused to play a similar role in a film called *Women Love Diamonds*. She also insisted that her $600 per week salary be increased to $5000. This was not such an unreasonable request, as Gilbert was earning $10,000 per week at the time. By 1936 she had become the highest-paid woman in the United States commanding a fee of $250,000 per film. Garbo's silent films established her as MGM's most prestigious asset and one of their leading box-office attractions with legions of adoring fans around the world.

Grand Hotel *(1932):*
In spite of the brevity of her appearance . . . Garbo dominates the picture entirely, making the other players merely competent performers . . . giving the tricky, clever film a lift, a spring, such as pictures without her, without that intense, nervous vitality she's got, cannot possess.
 John Mosher in the New Yorker, *1932*

The studio made her first talkie when the day could be put off no longer. It was a subject of as much concern to the company's stockholders as it was eagerly awaited by her fans.

She was 25 when she made her sound debut in 1930. Having risen on a string of clichéd plots, the choice of Eugene O'Neill's play *Anna Christie* had less to do with the fact that it was written by a great American playwright, than that Anna was Swedish, and thus Garbo's accent would be in character.

'Garbo talks!' shouted hoardings throughout the country. Her first spoken words – 'Gimme a visky, ginger ale on the side, and don't be stingy baby' – became much quoted that year.

Great care had been taken to ensure success, but as an extra precaution, since she was an enormous favourite in Europe, a simultaneous but different, grimly realistic German version was directed by the Belgian Jacques Feyder. Both were highly successful and her sub-

sequent pictures, though she made no more foreign versions, showed that her accent was no hindrance to the roles she played. She was English in *The Painted Veil* (1934); Russian in *Grand Hotel* (1932), *Anna Karenina* (1935) and *Ninotchka* (1939); Polish in *Conquest* (1937); Italian in *Romance* (1930) and *As You Desire Me* (1932); French in *Camille* (1936); a Dutch-Javanese spy in *Mata Hari* (1932) and American in *Susan Lenox: Her Fall and Rise* (1931). Reviewing *Romance*, the magazine *Picture-Play* commented:

'What matter if Garbo's accent only occasionally suggests the Italian's efforts to speak English? The Garbo voice itself is not of Italian quality or inflection, but for all anyone cares Rita Cavallini might as well be Portuguese or Rumanian, for it is her emotions that are conveyed by Garbo to the spectator.'
She spoke in the manner of her close-ups – with a voice that was dark, deep, and resonant.

Garbo's style was to some degree influenced by the celebrated Danish film star Asta Nielsen, with whom she starred in Berlin, and, later in America by Jeanne Eagels who was working at MGM when Garbo's own career was beginning to take shape. She shared with them a casual, almost off-hand delivery and a restless-

---

Anna Karenina *(1935):*
. . . It is Greta Garbo's personality which makes this film, which fills the mould of the neat respectful adaptation with some sense of the greatness of the novel. No other film actress can so convey physical passion that you believe in its importance, and yet there is no actress who depends so little on her own sexual charm.
 Graham Greene in the Spectator, *1935*

---

ness in manner and movement, epitomizing the spirit of a modern woman. Few of her films were ever totally satisfying in creating a suitable environment for her, but they all had their moments, such as her entrance in *Anna Karenina* when she appears to the waiting group on the train station through a cloud of mist and steam. In *Grand Hotel*, where she plays the ballerina Grusinskaya, she tells the jewel thief she loves, 'Is it money you want? I have money', with such guileless simplicity

Top: Garbo and Gable were passionately teamed in Susan Lenox: Her Fall and Rise, *but critics complained of the 'poorly developed episodes'.*
Left: Rouben Mamoulian told Garbo to make her face 'a blank sheet of paper' on which each member of the audience could write his own ending to Queen Christina.

that it becomes possible for him to refuse her offer, even though it will cost him his life. In *Mata Hari*, her manner of cupping a young officer's face in her hands for a kiss signifies a secret understanding, shared by the spectator, that by accepting a human love she also takes with it a human fate that will demand her sacrifice. *Queen Christina* (1933), Garbo's only film with Rouben Mamoulian, contains two of her most memorable scenes. The first occurs

---

Camille *(1936):*
Her own performance as Marguerite in- stilled humour and vitality into a flyblown romance . . . If she is capable of such creation, she should be appearing on her own account in roles which she alone can play. But perhaps her magic is only a freak of nature which leads our imagination to make of her an ideal which she can never be.
Cecil Beaton's Scrapbook, *1937*

---

when, alone with her lover at the inn, she wanders about their bedroom delicately touch- ing the furniture, in order to fix the room forever in her memory. The other scene is the film's finale: Christina, her lover dead, moves to the prow of the ship, bound for Spain. As music swells to a crescendo, the camera holds Garbo's immobile face in one long close-up – an unforgettable illustration of the power of her countenance to awake and suggest emotions in the audience.

Critically, she was unassailable. The New York Film Critics twice gave her their award of best actress for *Anna Karenina* and *Camille*. Writers composed great speeches for her and so began to limit her to the depths in her voice at the expense of the vistas opened up by her

gestures; the sort of films that would have created opportunities for visually expressive acting failed to materialize. Typical of the films in which she was cast was *Conquest*, a lavish saga that ran two hours and had only a few dramatic moments. By the end of the decade she had become a cliché of doom – poetic, tragic, but unwelcome. This distanced her from a public who had seen in her, and required of her, more than that.

Ninotchka *(1939):*
Garbo's Ninotchka is one of the sprightliest comedies of the year, a gay and impertinent and malicious show which never pulls the punch lines (no matter how far below the belt they land) and finds the screen's first lady of drama playing in a deadpan comedy with the assurance of a Buster Keaton . . .
Frank S. Nugent
in the New York Times, *1939*

Garbo's career could have gone on, had she wished, but to remain at the top she would have needed the box-office authority to get her own way, and that would have required a change of image from the stereotype she had become.

Realizing the necessity for a change of tack, MGM took the risk of casting her in a comedy, directed by Ernst Lubitsch, called *Ninotchka*. The advertising proclaimed 'Garbo laughs!' as once it had promised 'Garbo talks!' – despite the fact that she had been laughing in her films for more than ten years. The studio's gamble paid off, however – audiences rapturously received her first American light role, hailing her as past mistress of comedy.

Ninotchka was a box-office hit, Garbo's first for some years. It encouraged MGM to cast her in a second comedy, *Two-Faced Woman* (1941). It was severely mauled by the critics – *Time* called it 'An absurd vehicle for Greta Garbo . . . its embarrassing effect is not unlike seeing Sarah Bernhardt swatted with a bladder.'

On completing *Two-Faced Woman*, Garbo took a sabbatical. It was never to end.

Rumours persisted about the films she might appear in as they did about romances she supposedly had, but she neither married nor returned to the screen.

Only once did she appear before a movie camera – for a silent, black-and-white makeup test that she made in 1948 for the proposed Max Ophuls version of *La Duchesse de Langeais*. In take after take she moves her head from side to side with no more animation than a slightly bemused smile on her lips. There seems to be nothing of interest until, near the end of the reel, the off-screen cameraman apparently asks her to remove her distracting little skull cap. In compliance, her hands go up into frame as her head tilts back; something he said must have amused her, for she laughs. And the small screen lights up – one is excited and expectant. There was magic, without the aid of lines or even the simplest of motivations. Better than anything, it reveals the one thing about her – her ability to transcend what people wrote for her and what she acted in. The only screenwriter Garbo needed was the camera, and the camera produced the legend.

JOHN KOBAL

Filmography
1920 En Lyckoriddare (extra). '**21** Herr och Fru Stockholm (adv film). '**22** Konsumtionsföreni- ngen Stockholm med omnejd (adv film); Luffar- Petter (USA/GB: Peter the Tramp). '**24** Gösta Berlings Saga (USA/GB: The Atonement of Gösta Berling/The Legend of Gösta Berling). '**25** Die Freudlose Gasse (GER) (USA: Streets of Sorrow, reissued with post-synchronized sound in 1937 as The Street of Sorrow; GB: The Joyless Street). *All remaining films USA unless specified:* '**26** The Torrent; The Temptress. '**27** Flesh and the Devil; Love (trade-shown in GB as Anna Karenina). '**28** The Divine Woman; The Mysterious Lady; A Woman of Affairs. '**29** Wild Orchids; A Man's Man (as herself); The Kiss; The Single Standard. '**30** Anna Christie (English version); Anna Christie (German version); Romance. '**31** Inspiration; Susan Lenox: Her Fall and Rise (GB: The Rise of Helga). '**32** Mata Hari; Grand Hotel; As You Desire Me. '**33** Queen Christina. '**34** The Painted Veil. '**35** Anna Karenina. '**36** Camille. '**37** Conquest (GB: Marie Walewska). '**39** Ninotchka. '**41** Two-Faced Woman.

I could go on singing

**'I'm sick and tired of being called "poor Judy Garland".
Maybe this will distress a lot of people but I've got an
awfully nice life. I really have. I like to laugh. I like to
have a bag of popcorn and go on a roller-coaster now and
then. I wouldn't have been able to learn a song if I'd been
as sick as they've printed me all the time'**

Judy Garland

Judy Garland is one of the great legends of the movies; yet paradoxically, considerably less than half of her professional career – which occupied the best part of 44 of her 47 years of life – was spent in films. The intervening periods were taken up with her ever-growing and unkindly publicized personal problems. She was impatient with the view, constantly expressed by the popular press, that she was a show business tragedy. On one occasion she confided: 'People say and print and believe – the stupid ones, and that's the minority – that I'm either a drunk or a drug addict. It's a goddam wonder I'm not.'

She was born Frances Gumm in Grand Rapids, Minnesota, on June 10, 1922. Her parents, Frank and Ethel Gumm, had had a vaudeville act for a while before they settled in the movie business. Her father became a cinema proprietor and her mother – bent perhaps on fulfilling her own thwarted ambitions through her children – had formed the two older daughters into a sister act that performed in the vaudeville part of the cinema's shows. As legend has it, Baby Gumm (as the adored and spoiled youngest child was known) made her debut when she was around two and a half years old, bringing the house down with a rendering of 'Jingle Bells'; with great delight

she encored repeatedly until she was dragged off, struggling, by her father. She had tasted, for the first time, the adulation of audiences which was, it seemed, eventually to become a necessary drug like all the rest. Unsatisfied, she was later to confide: 'Being Judy Garland – sure I've been loved by the public. I can't take the public home with me . . .'

When they moved to California, the whole family had to work in vaudeville – the parents as Frank and Virginia Lee and the children as the Gumm Sisters – to eke out the meagre takings of the new cinema.

It soon became clear that Baby Gumm was the star, even though one unfeeling manager advised her: 'You may sing loud but you don't sing good'. At six she had a solo spot at Loews' State Theatre in Los Angeles, singing 'I Can't Give You Anything but Love', dressed as Cupid. With so precocious a repertoire and technique and so loud a voice, it was hardly surprising that audiences paid her the dubious compliment of suspecting she was a midget.

When she was 11 she changed her name. The Gumm girls had been rushed into a vaudeville bill in Chicago to replace a drop-out act – and arrived to find that they had been billed as 'The Glum Sisters'. The compere of the show was George Jessel, who persuaded them

Top left: Judy Garland waiting in the wings of the London Palladium. Top: 'Dear Mr Gable' convinced MGM of her gifts. Above: in the MGM canteen are, from left to right, Deanna Durbin, Judy Garland and Jackie Cooper.

that it was not a good stage name anyway and proposed Garland instead. A little later, Frances took the name 'Judy' from a current Hoagy Carmichael hit song.

Mrs Gumm had battled, without success, to get her children into movies. Their only appearance had been with a troupe of other infant performers, the Meglin Kiddies, in a 1929 short – *The Old Lady and the Shoe*. In 1934, however, Judy Garland acquired an agent, Al Rosen, and at least one admirer within MGM, Joseph Mankiewicz. Between them they managed to arrange an audition. The story is a show business legend – how Judy was summoned at such short notice that she had not even time to change out of her play clothes or do her hair.

No doubt this impromptu and informal appearance enhanced the child's open and appealing personality. She made sufficient impression on Ida Koverman, Louis B. Mayer's influential secretary, and Jack Robbins, the company's talent chief, for them to bring in the studio rehearsal pianist, Roger Edens, and send for Mayer himself. Mayer, who was harassed by the current internecine struggles of the company, came reluctantly. He listened without a word and a few days later offered a contract – unprecedentedly without asking for a screen test.

The MGM days began inauspiciously with the sudden death of Frank Gumm, which can hardly have helped Judy Garland's emotional and psychological development. Despite this, she was later to say that the first days were 'a lot of laughs'. Labour laws required the studio to give its children adequate schooling and Garland found herself in a class-room with

Right: Mickey Rooney and Judy Garland falling in love over ice-cream sodas in Love Finds Andy Hardy. *Bottom: MGM promoted their singing and dancing duo – Garland and Rooney – as 'the most popular young movie stars in the world'. Bottom right: Judy Garland as Dorothy with her dog Toto in the film that firmly established her in the hearts of the public –* The Wizard of Oz

Lana Turner, Jackie Cooper, Deanna Durbin, Freddie Bartholomew and other youthful actors. With Durbin she was teamed in a short, *Every Sunday* (1936), which was so unpromising that Durbin's option was dropped (she was triumphantly snatched up and made into a star by Universal) and Garland was loaned to 20th Century-Fox for *Pigskin Parade* (1936), a college musical in which she sang three songs, hated herself for looking like 'a fat little pig with pigtails' and won one or two favourable notices.

The studio still had no plans for her; it was Roger Edens who conceived the ruse that finally convinced MGM what a treasure they had on their hands. Clark Gable's thirty-sixth birthday was celebrated with a studio party on the set of *Parnell* (1937) and Edens devised a special treatment of 'You Made Me Love You' with Garland doing a monologue, 'Dear Mr Gable', in the character of a devoted admirer writing a fan letter. Gable was greatly touched and Garland was launched. MGM at once put her – and Edens' 'Dear Mr Gable' number – into *Broadway Melody of 1938* (1937).

She then co-starred with Mickey Rooney,

with whom she found an instant sympathy, in *Thoroughbreds Don't Cry* (1937) and with another school-fellow, Freddie Bartholomew, in *Listen, Darling* (1938) – in which the two youngsters kidnap the widowed Mary Astor and take her on a search for a suitable husband. In *Everybody Sing* (1938) she appeared alongside the great Broadway veteran, Fanny Brice.

In all of these films Garland sang, for the public had already succumbed to the extraordinary voice. It was thrillingly strident (as a child she had been disrespectfully dubbed 'Little Miss Leather Lungs') with a heart-rending catch, miraculously expressive and, even in those early days, so mature that she was able to give convincing interpretations of the great torch songs like Fanny Brice's 'My Man'. The musical staff at MGM, where the gifted Arthur Freed was already the dominant influence, wisely preferred to exploit the vivacity and humour of her gifts in songs like 'Swing, Mr Mendelssohn' and 'Zing Went the Strings of My Heart'.

Garland was teamed with MGM's most popular juvenile, Mickey Rooney, in the Andy

Above: Judy Garland was given a major adult part for the first time when she played a vaudeville performer caught up in World War I in For Me and My Gal. *Above right: on the set of* Meet Me in St Louis, *in which she plays the romantic Esther; it was directed by her future husband Vincente Minnelli. Right: with Robert Walker in the wartime romance* The Clock

Hardy series which acquired a new musical flavour. Garland acted and sang in three of the series – *Love Finds Andy Hardy* (1938), *Andy Hardy Meets Debutante* (1940) and *Life Begins for Andy Hardy* (1941) – although the studio saw fit to remove Garland's songs from the release print of the last of these.

This series was interrupted by the film which firmly and finally established Garland as a major star and gave her the theme tune which she sang and continually enriched until the end of her life – 'Over the Rainbow'. L. Frank Baum's series of Oz books for children had begun to appear in 1900 and had become best-sellers. A silent version of *The Wizard of Oz* had been made in 1925 with Larry Semon and Oliver Hardy. MGM were prepared to lavish colour and $2 million on a new version. They also intended to lavish Shirley Temple on it but, when she was not available, Garland was accepted as a second choice. There was difficulty and indecision over directors, but credit for *The Wizard of Oz* (1939) finally went to Victor Fleming as it did for *Gone With the Wind* (also 1939). The script was intelligent, the technical achievement high and the cast distinguished; but it was Judy Garland's picture.

Audiences adored Garland – as they were to go on doing – for her vitality, her gaiety, her openness, her intimacy and the generous, friendly, loving nature in her. But behind the scenes life was taking on a darker aspect. Her irrepressible *joie de vivre* included a hearty appetite; but the malted milks and Hershey bars to which she was addicted made her fat. Mayer himself laid down what she might eat (mostly chicken soup) and what she might not.

She discovered, among other evidence of the studio's parental care for her, that the lifelong friend with whom she had moved into a bachelor apartment, had become a company spy, paid to report on her every move. So, it transpired, was her own mother.

To help her fight off the pangs of hunger she was given the newly fashionable drug Benzedrine. To counteract its over-stimulant effects, she was given sleeping pills; to wake her up again, more stimulants and then other pills to calm her nerves. Despite all the later efforts of her friends and publicists to play down the inevitable effects of all this 'medication', the dependence was to become a nightmare and culminated in her death due to an accidental drug overdose.

The public could not have enough of her and the company worked her mercilessly. She was threatened with the fate that had afflicted Mary Pickford 20 years before: public and studio would not let her grow up. When she played the dual role of a girl and her mother in *Little Nellie Kelly* (1940), Mayer is said to have gone around wailing, 'We can't let that baby have a baby'. Mayer and the studio did not hide their displeasure when, in 1941, Garland married orchestra leader David Rose and it is certain that they did nothing to ward off the rapid break-up of the marriage.

In the next three years Garland appeared in a number of attractive musicals – *Ziegfeld Girl* (1941), *For Me and My Gal* (1942), *Presenting Lily Mars* and *Thousands Cheer* (both 1943).

In 1944 came *Meet Me in St Louis*, still the most cheering and charming of all the MGM musicals, in which Garland sings some of her most memorable songs. Her dramatic talent – about which she continued to have doubts – had become much more refined: her great achievement in this film is to subsume herself into the whole ensemble of finely cast actors portraying an ordinary family of 1904 and the excitements of the great St Louis Exposition.

The director of *Meet Me in St Louis* was Vincente Minnelli, whom she married – this time with the studio's delighted approval – in July 1945. In March of the following year their daughter Liza was born. She was delivered by Caesarian section which added to the growing

strains on Garland's health. Minnelli directed her in her first non-musical role, *The Clock* (1945), a short episode in the *Ziegfeld Follies* (1946) and in the wonderfully inventive *The Pirate* (1948) in which her co-star was the young Gene Kelly.

But the strain was taking its toll. The studio showed scant patience with her illnesses, her unpunctuality and absences and her growing nerviness. She was sick during the making of *The Pirate* and hospitalized after it. MGM planned a new Garland–Kelly musical but Kelly had an accident and was replaced by Fred Astaire in *Easter Parade* (1948), one of Garland's gayest films. A further Astaire–Garland vehicle was frustrated when she was replaced due to illness in *The Barkleys of Broadway* (1949). Without pause, however, she went into *Words and Music* (1948), a musical biography of Rogers and Hart, and *In the Good Old Summertime* (1949), a musical remake of *The Shop Around the Corner* (1940). Exhausted, she managed to record songs for *Annie Get Your Gun* (1950), but when filming began she was replaced as 'unreliable'.

Weak and sick she struggled through *Summer Stock* (1950), although on the screen she is as vital, as irresistibly cheerful as at any time in her career: the audience detects nothing of the intolerable exhaustion. After this she was, for once, herself called upon to replace another star: June Allyson was having a baby and could not do *Royal Wedding* (1951). Garland recorded the songs but then fell ill. MGM suspended her and her days with the company that, from her fourteenth year, had appointed itself her parent and family and keeper, were over.

The next four years saw her start a new career as a variety and concert performer. On April 9, 1951 she began a season at the London Palladium and in October of the same year she launched into a 19-week season at the Palace, New York, which is now regarded as vaudeville history. Again the strain proved too great for her and she missed several performances from illness.

Divorced from Minnelli, she married Sidney Luft, by whom she had two more children – Lorna and Joey – and with whom she formed a

production company, Transcona. For Warner Brothers, Transcona made *A Star Is Born* (1954), directed by George Cukor – who had style and taste and appreciation of both the talent and problems of an artist like Garland. The film was brutally manhandled by the studio who cut it extensively and then added new material (which, at least, included the memorable 'Born in a Trunk' number). This somewhat hoary sob story, about a Hollywood marriage between a rising star (the girl) and a falling meteor, had been filmed originally in 1936 by William Wellman with Fredric March and Janet Gaynor. In Cukor's hands it acquired new life and depth: at one level it poignantly echoed Garland's own real-life problems with Hollywood; at another, there was never any difficulty in believing in her as a star of supreme status.

Her role in *A Star Is Born* is perhaps her best and she certainly gave her most moving and dramatic performance. For all practical purposes it marked the end of her film career. She had a single impressive scene in Stanley Kramer's *Judgement at Nuremberg* (1961). *A Child Is Waiting* (1963), a low-pitched, appealing film about a home for sub-normal children, echoed, in Garland's touching scenes with the children, her hospital periods in which she had found relief in working and playing with child patients.

She had by this time developed a great liking for London, where she made *I Could Go on Singing* (dir. Ronald Neame, 1963). The film was an undistinguished melodrama with musical numbers but the theme – the struggle between a singing star and her husband (Dirk

Top: I Could Go on Singing, *the story of a famous singer who tries to reclaim her son from her ex-husband, had sad echoes of Garland's own life. Above: surrounded by retarded children in* A Child is Waiting

Bogarde) for possession of their children – was uncomfortably close to life. Garland was suing for divorce from Sidney Luft and their wrangles over the children added to the unattractive publicity Garland was to receive in her few remaining years.

The fans who crowded the concerts which were to be her work from this time on were more and more enthusiastic, more and more demanding. From her own account, she derived some sort of comfort from this public affection. Her private life became more difficult. After earning an estimated $8 million, mismanagement had left her with nothing but crippling debts. Her health progressively worsened. Non-appearances and tragically incapable performances, along with a short-lived marriage to Mark Herron, the struggles with Luft over the children, breach of contract suits and other major or minor misfortunes, invariably gathered publicity.

To the end, though, she could still suddenly snap back into form to excite her audiences as few other performers have done and then move them (and herself) to real tears as she sat on the edge of the stage, suddenly transported back in time, once again little Dorothy from *The Wizard of Oz*, singing – huskily and hopefully – 'Over the Rainbow'.

The end came unexpectedly. Garland had married actor Mickey Deane, and in the brief period that they were together seemed calm and happy, although by this time she was

terribly thin and her face showed, more than ever before, the strains of time. On the morning of June 22, 1969 her husband found her dead in their London apartment; her death, it seems, caused by an accidental overdose of sleeping pills.

'She was a lady', James Mason, her co-star in *A Star Is Born* said at her funeral, 'who gave so much and richly both to her vast audience whom she entertained and to the friends around her whom she loved that there was no currency in which to repay her. And she needed to be repaid, she needed devotion and love beyond the resources of any of us.'

DAVID ROBINSON

Filmography

1929 The Old Lady and the Shoe (short) **'35** La Fiesta de Santa Barbara (short). **'36** Every Sunday (short); Pigskin Parade (GB: The Harmony Parade). **'37** Broadway Melody of 1938; Thoroughbreds Don't Cry. **'38** Everybody Sing; Listen, Darling; Love Finds Andy Hardy. **'39** The Wizard of Oz; Babes in Arms. **'40** Andy Hardy Meets Debutante (GB: Andy Hardy Meets a Debutante); Strike Up the Band; Little Nellie Kelly. **'41** Ziegfeld Girl; Meet the People (short); Life Begins for Andy Hardy; Babes on Broadway. **'42** For Me and My Gal (GB: For Me and My Girl). **'43** Presenting Lily Mars; Girl Crazy; Thousands Cheer. **'44** Meet Me in St Louis. **'45** The Clock (GB: Under the Clock). **'46** The Harvey Girls; Ziegfeld Follies; Till the Clouds Roll By. **'48** The Pirate; Easter Parade; Words and Music. **'49** In the Good Old Summertime. **'50** Summer Stock (GB: If You Feel Like Singing). **'54** A Star Is Born. 'Pepe (voice only). **'61** Judgement at Nuremberg. **'62** Gay Puree (voice only). **'63** A Child Is Waiting; I Could Go on Singing (GB).

Top: even under great strain Judy Garland could always look glamorous. Above: she relaxes while shooting A Star Is Born *with two of her children – Lorna Luft (in her arms) and Liza Minnelli, aged seven*

JEAN HARLOW

Jean Harlow, the 'Platinum Blonde', was one of Hollywood's flashiest sex symbols. She always portrayed seductive sirens. These had an innocent, animal quality in her early roles and an air of tart sophistication in her later ones. Because she died when she was 26, she appears an ageless incarnation of sex to modern moviegoers. In real life, regardless of what certain unscrupulous biographers may have written, she was trusting and naive, with an instinctive talent for comedy.

The girl from Missouri

She was born in Kansas City, Missouri, and christened Harlean. Her father, Dr Montclair Carpenter and her mother, whose name was originally Jean Harlow, split up before their daughter reached her teens. Harlean had a twangy voice, unblemished skin and a beautifully rounded body. Adopting her mother's maiden name, she began work as an extra in silent films; her film debut occurred in Chicago in 1926 when she was 15. That year she eloped with Charles McGrew for a brief, passionless marriage that failed to survive parental displeasure.

By that time, Jean's mother had married a florid dandy with loud ways named Marino Bello. Although he claimed to be a successful business man, he was most successful at meddling in Jean's life. Her dislike for him was matched by her love for her mother and these conflicting emotions created constant discord in the Bello home.

In the late Twenties, the family moved to California. Hollywood was a Mecca for the world's most beautiful girls. Even against that competition, Jean's attractiveness was spectacular, but though she worked regularly in films, proper recognition eluded her until Howard Hughes gave her the lead in his talking version of *Hell's Angels* (1930). This flying epic lifted her to instant stardom.

The impact she made in *Hell's Angels* was short-lived. Although audiences appreciated her flip personality and platinum blonde locks, her acting was less well received. She drew loud guffaws everywhere when, attired in a thin, revealing dress, she asked the hero, 'Would you be shocked if I slip into something more comfortable?' But it was her sexy appearance that wrought the damage, enraging puritans, women's clubs and censor boards. To escape their wrath, producers chose other actresses for roles ideally suited to Harlow.

Red-haired dynamite

Howard Hughes held her to a contract but neglected her when casting subsequent films. She was sent plummeting from instant stardom to near-instant oblivion. She engaged in a series of disastrous personal appearances in the American Midwest and along the Atlantic seaboard, until MGM producer Paul Bern persuaded his boss, Irving Thalberg, that she would be an asset to their cinematic constellation. Her contract was bought from Hughes and she soared to new prominence when, dark-wigged, she starred in Bern's production of *Red-Headed Woman* (1932) – a film that not only incurred the wrath of her existing critics but created new ones. Defying them, MGM

Right: Jean Harlow, flagrantly clad in furs and skin-clinging gown, was a head-turning status symbol every Thirties American male dreamed of possessing

THE BLONDE BOMBSHELL

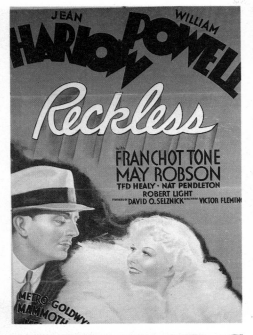

continued Harlow's rejuvenated career.

Harlow took all this in her stride. She was likeable, happy-go-lucky, and now suddenly successful. Her frank, outgoing personality contrasted with the mild, intellectual Bern. But more than a mutual interest in film-making drew them together and they were soon married. Then, two months after the wedding, Bern shot himself.

Harlow was never involved in the controversy that followed. Although touched by his death, she threw herself into film after film, starring in a dozen MGM movies in less than four years. Some, like *Red Dust* (1932), *Bombshell*, *Dinner at Eight* (both 1933), *China Seas* (1935) and *Libeled Lady* (1936), reveal a comedienne who rates with the screen's best.

She married cinematographer Hal Rosson a year after Bern's suicide. Like her late husband, Rosson was short, quiet, intellectual and devoted to her and her career. But her second marriage was also short-lived, ending in divorce after only six months.

Beautiful losers

During 1934, Harlow completed a semi-erotic novel called *Today Is Tonight*. MGM, always watchdogging the image of its stars, purchased every available copy and the film rights. The embarrassing work was quickly filed away and forgotten.

Harlow's last love was William Powell, urbane on and off screen and her co-star in *Reckless* (1935) and *Libeled Lady*. He was the former husband of Carole Lombard, who was popular, like Jean, as a sexy comedienne. The Harlow/Powell affair was hectic and quarrelsome. When it broke up, Jean became ill, contracting a dangerous kidney disease. Severely depressed, she seemed not to care what happened to her. Her mother, a devoted Christian Scientist, tried to effect a cure without recourse to medicine but failed, and Jean died of uremic poisoning.

In life and death, Jean Harlow, Carole Lombard and Marilyn Monroe were counterparts. All three were blonde and beautiful, and all three were fated to die young and needlessly.

SAMUEL MARX

Filmography
1928 Moran of the Marines; Double Whoopee (short); The Unkissed Man (short). **'29** Close Harmony; New York Nights; The Love Parade; The Saturday Night Kid; Weak but Willing. **'30** Hell's Angels. **'31** The Secret Six; The Iron Man; The Public Enemy (GB: Enemies of the Public); City Lights; Goldie; Platinum Blonde. **'32** Three Wise Girls; The Beast of the City; Red-Headed Woman; Red Dust. **'33** Hold Your Man; Bombshell (GB: Blonde Bombshell); Dinner at Eight. **'34** The Girl From Missouri (GB: 100 Per Cent Pure). **'35** Reckless; China Seas. **'36** Riffraff; Wife vs Secretary; Suzy; Libeled Lady. **'37** Personal Property (GB: The Man in Possession); Saratoga (died during filming; a double replaced her in some scenes).

Harlow's leading men ranged from the debonair William Powell in Reckless *(top far left) to the wild James Cagney in* The Public Enemy *(bottom left), and included Spencer Tracy in* Riffraff *(top left), Wallace Beery in* Dinner at Eight *(centre left) and Ben Lyon in* Hell's Angels *(centre far left). Clark Gable, here in* Red Dust *(bottom far left), was her most frequent partner*

Lovely Rita

Woman of mystery or happy-go-lucky girl-next-door? Rita Hayworth somehow blended the attributes of both in her screen personality. The result was irresistible

In John Huston's madly haphazard but inspired *Beat the Devil* (1953), Humphrey Bogart is led off by Arabs to a seemingly certain death. When next seen, however, he is in cosy conversation with the local sheikh who smiles benignly and says, 'And so you really know the lovely Rita?' while behind him hang dozens of glittering photographs of the star. The joke would not have been half as amusing had it not been founded on fact. From the Gulf of Aden to Brooklyn (where she was born in 1918), Rita Hayworth was *the* love goddess of films, the incarnation of eroticism in the post-war years.

That image of the free-living, sleekly sophisticated, sexual animal – fully realized for the first time in *Gilda* (1946) – was, nonetheless, consciously created by Hayworth and various collaborators, and was almost a decade in the making. In spite of her apparent defiance of convention – her much publicized series of marriages, divorces and romances – Hayworth and her co-workers have often denied that the image has much connection with her real personality. This denial is summed up by her

Above: this publicity shot of Hayworth taken in the early Fifties bears out Orson Welles' comment that 'she was one of those whom the camera loved and rendered immortal'. Right: in her first A film – Only Angels Have Wings

most oft-quoted statement. In an attempt to explain the failure of several of her marriages she once said: 'They all married Gilda, but they woke up with me.'

The lovely señorita

Hayworth started her career as a rather dumpy 13-year-old, dancing with her then-famous father Eduardo under her real name, Margarita Carmen Cansino, in various nightclubs, primarily in Mexico. Trained by her father, she became an accomplished dancer, especially to Latin rhythms. Joseph Cotten once commented later that 'no matter how bad the rest of the film, when Rita started to dance it was like seeing one of nature's wonders in motion.'

She was discovered by Hollywood in 1933. Warner Brothers turned her down after a test because she was overweight and her hairline was too low, but Winfield Sheenan, head of production at Fox, signed her; he was impressed with the way she held herself and her grace of movement. As Rita Cansino she danced briefly in a club sequence in *Dante's Inferno* (1935) and appeared in four mediocre films. When Fox merged with 20th Century Films, the new head of production, Darryl F. Zanuck, replaced her in the title role of the Technicolor *Ramona* (1936) with Loretta Young, and then cancelled her contract.

Hayworth freelanced her way through the tepid *Meet Nero Wolfe* (1936) and four forgettable Westerns.

Those of her admirers who claim with hindsight to be able to perceive all Hayworth's later qualities in those early appearances do her a disservice by disregarding the years of hard work and professional craftsmanship which made her a star. In these first films she was adequate in parts that called for little. The profile was there, as was a certain exuberance, but not much more.

A head start

Her husband, Edward C. Judson, then took a hand in her career. He insisted that she take diction lessons, put her on a diet, changed her makeup and way of dressing, and sent her to an electrolysist to have her hairline raised, therby broadening her forehead. Harry Cohn, boss of Columbia studios, saw her and liked what he saw. He signed her at $250-a-week (to rise to $1750 over seven years), changed her name – in part to conceal her past film work – and put her in a dozen programmers to let her gain experience and to find out what might be made of her. She was ambitious, patient and anxious to learn. When a good part in a good film came along, she was ready for it.

She got her chance in Howard Hawks' *Only Angels Have Wings* (1939). She was cast as the second female lead, playing Richard Barthelmess' flighty but ultimately loyal wife. She was good enough to be noticed by audiences and critics, and at least held her own with Cary Grant and Jean Arthur, the film's two main stars. George Cukor, a director with a keen instinct for a talented actress, had tested Hayworth in 1938 for the female lead in *Holiday* (subsequently given to Katharine Hepburn), but had felt she was too inexperienced. He remembered her, however, and borrowed her from Columbia for MGM's *Susan and God* (1940), starring Joan Crawford. Her role was not large but it was glamorous. The public quickly responded. Columbia began to churn out publicity photographs to satisfy her growing following; Cohn was aware that he had found a star, but he was not sure quite what to do with her.

He tried her in two A films: *The Lady in*

Question, (1940), which was the first time Hayworth was directed by Charles Vidor who would later collaborate on three of her biggest hits, and *Angels Over Broadway* (1940). The reviews were good, including those for Hayworth, but neither film did much business. Two other studios then showed Cohn Hayworth's real possibilities.

Warner Brothers had planned *The Strawberry Blonde* (1941) for Ann Sheridan. When she refused to do it at the last moment, the studio looked for an available second-level star whose size and colouring (in spite of the film being shot in black and white) would fit the costumes designed for Sheridan. Hayworth, who dyed her black hair to its now famous red, was thus given the role of the sunny gold digger out to steal dentist James Cagney from nice Olivia de Havilland. The film was a smash, as was Hayworth. After a minor comedy at Warners she was then loaned to 20th Century-Fox to replace Carole Landis (who refused to dye her hair red or to play an unsympathetic part) in Mamoulian's Technicolor *Blood and Sand* (1941). As Dona Sol, the noblewoman-temptress who temporarily steals bullfighter Tyrone Power from Linda Darnell, Hayworth was ravishing to look at. The film, quite rightly, was not very popular, but Hayworth received a great deal of attention. Between 1941 and 1942, her face appeared on the front cover of 23 magazines.

Naughty but nice
Although she played an unfaithful wife in one episode of Ben Hecht's *Tales of Manhattan* (1942), it was the lighter side of her role in *The Strawberry Blonde* that was emphasized in five films over the next four years – during which she established herself as a major star. She managed to be beautiful and erotic, in a 'nice' way – a girl-next-door whom women could admire and not worry if their men admired her as well, for she was never a conscious threat. She also returned to her origins as a dancer, becoming connected in the mind of her public with musicals. Until the late Fifties, audiences would eagerly await her big

Top: a young dentist (Cagney) manages to get a date with the girl of his dreams in The Strawberry Blonde. *Above, far right: Hayworth (left) in the musical* Down to Earth. *Right: both she and her then husband Orson Welles look pleased with her new, short, blonde hair-do created for* The Lady From Shanghai.

number(s) no matter what kind of film she was appearing in. Unfortunately her singing voice was weak, so that her songs were always dubbed (a closely guarded secret during her Columbia days). *You'll Never Get Rich* (1941) and *You Were Never Lovelier* (1942) had everything that musicals of the time needed for success – except colour – including songs by Cole Porter (for the former) and Jerome Kern (for the latter), with Fred Astaire appearing in both.

The plot of *Cover Girl* (1944) is silly and clichéd (will girl dancer make it on talent or beauty, remain with the poor dancer who loves her or run off with a wealthy playboy?), but that hardly matters, even when the film is seen today. Never more beautiful in colour (cameraman Rudolph Maté worked with Hayworth on her next four films and remained her favourite), she was teamed with Gene Kelly and 'sang' and danced to songs by Kern and Ira Gershwin. The film was the biggest hit of Hayworth's career up to then.

Down to Earth (1947) was planned before the release of *Gilda* and put into production just 18 days before that film's release. In it she plays a goddess (Terpsichore, the muse of dancing) who comes down to earth to help a young stage producer (Larry Parks) succeed on Broadway. The film was lavishly shot in colour, Hayworth looked beautiful and the

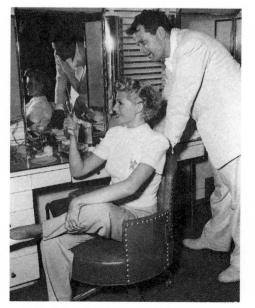

box-offices did good business. But the film was overshadowed by *Gilda*, which had provided Hayworth with a new image more in keeping with the prevailing attitudes of post-war America. She had also discovered a new maturity as an actress. As the far-from-innocent *film noir* 'heroine' she was asked to do a good deal more than simply look beautiful and dance well. Although she would appear, from time to time, in less demanding roles in indifferent films, from *Gilda* until *The Money Trap* (1965), there is a seriousness of intent and achievement in Hayworth as an actress often overlooked by critics.

The thrill is gone
After *Gilda*, Hayworth's career slowly began to fade. She continued to have box-office hits for another seven years, but much of the excitement and erotic charge of *Gilda* was lacking. During those seven years, however, she made one of her finest films with her then husband Orson Welles, *The Lady From Shanghai* (1947). It was a financial failure when it was first released, partially because it was a

Welles film and not a Hayworth vehicle: her hair was cut and bleached; there were no dances (and just one, ironic, song); and her character did not even have the sympathetic qualities that Gilda had possessed. Yet, with *Gilda*, it is vintage Hayworth, and one of the finest films Hollywood made in the Forties. *The Lady From Shanghai* cuts through every romantic illusion and 'civilized' institution on which American society rests. The film was years ahead of its time, and Hayworth rightly regards it as one of the best things with which she has ever been associated.

Under a new Columbia contract (in which she stipulated that she must always be presented sympathetically on screen), she became a fun-loving, misunderstood Carmen in *The Loves of Carmen* (1948), beautiful (in colour) but unconvincing (especially with a wooden Glenn Ford as her Don José). She returned to the screen after an absence of four years (during which she married and separated from Aly Khan) in *Affair in Trinidad* (1952), a faded remake of *Gilda*. Entering the then popular biblical sweepstakes, she played a sympathetic, misunderstood *Salome* (1953) who dances to *save* John the Baptist. In the same year, obviously fighting a weight problem but full of a mature sexuality, she played *Miss Sadie Thompson* in colour and 3-D. The inferior and splashy *Salome* made money, the delightfully trashy *Miss Sadie Thompson* did not.

At odds with Cohn, she turned down a project entitled *Joseph and his Brethren*, but made *Fire Down Below* (1957) playing very much third string to Robert Mitchum and Jack Lemmon. After her role as an older woman who loses Frank Sinatra to Kim Novak in *Pal Joey* (1957), she left Columbia (although in 1959 she did an interesting Western, *They Came to Cordura*, for the studio).

Right: Hayworth freshens up in Pal Joey, *which marked the end of a distinguished musical career. Below: GIs drool and Hayworth looks cool in* Miss Sadie Thompson, *one of several versions of Somerset Maugham's* Rain. *Bottom: Hayworth and Gary Cooper in a tender moment from* They Came to Cordura

'Zip', her delightful tongue-in-cheek strip in *Pal Joey*, also marked the end of her musical days. She now turned to drama as an ageing actress (*Separate Tables*, 1958), a suffering wife on trial for murder (*The Story on Page One*, 1959), and a suffering mother (*Circus World*, 1964), and to comedy (*The Happy Thieves*, 1962). The first was popular and got good reviews; the rest were failures with the critics and the public (although Hayworth herself was not bad in any of them). The old romantic team of Hayworth and Glenn Ford worked well in *The Money Trap*; the director, Burt Kennedy, generated a good deal of excitement in their scenes together. In the film, a dishonest cop (Ford) visits his old flame (Hayworth) who has fallen on hard times. Still beautiful, Hayworth fills her brief scenes with pain and an undercurrent of still-smouldering eroticism. The film was a commercial failure; when it was released for TV, Hayworth's intelligent performance had been cut for time. That, unfortunately, is the print which re-entered theatrical distribution.

Since then, Hayworth has worked in half a

dozen low budget films in the USA, Italy and Spain. Two – *I Bastardi* (1968, *Sons of Satan*) and *Sur la Route de Salina* (1970, *Road to Salina*) – are of more than passing interest because of her fine performances of what are similar parts, a drunken ex-actress and a down-at-heel café owner. Hayworth is now in semi-retirement, although she occasionally appears at various festivals. Whether she will work again is a moot point. Although she is willing, it is unfortunately true that good parts for actresses of a 'certain age' are few. Nonetheless, if she never returns to the screen, a good many of us can sit contentedly in our tents and take pleasure in the fact that we once had the privilege of knowing 'the lovely Rita'.

DAVID OVERBEY

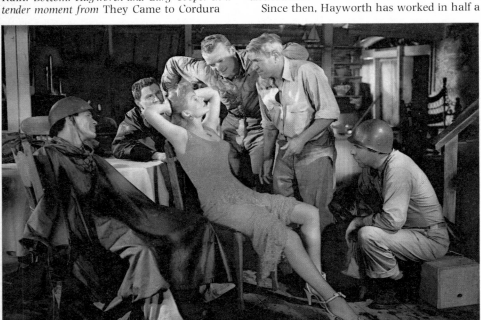

Filmography
1926 untitled short on folk dancing. **'35** Cruz Diablo (extra) (MEX); promotional film for studio Spanish-language versions (short); Under the Pampas Moon; Charlie Chan in Egypt; Dante's Inferno; Paddy O'Day. **'36** Human Cargo; Meet Nero Wolfe; Rebellion. **'37** Trouble in Texas; Old Louisiana/Louisiana Girl (GB: Treason); Hit the Saddle. **'37** Criminals of the Air; Girls Can Play; The Game That Kills; Paid to Dance (USA retitling for TV: Hard To Hold); The Shadow (GB: The Circus Shadow.) **'38** Who Killed Gail Preston?; There's Always a Woman; Convicted (CAN); Juvenile Court; The Renegade Ranger (CAN). **'39** Homicide Bureau; The Lone Wolf Spy Hunt (GB: The Lone Wolf's Daughter); Special Inspector (CAN); Only Angels Have Wings. **'40** Music in My Heart; Blondie on a Budget; Susan and God (GB: The Gay Mrs Trexel); The Lady in Question; Angels Over Broadway. **'41** The Strawberry Blonde; Affectionately Yours; Blood and Sand; You'll Never Get Rich. **'42** My Gal Sal; Tales of Manhattan; You Were Never Lovelier. **'43** Show Business at War (short). **'44** Cover Girl. **'45** Tonight and Every Night. **'46** Gilda. **'47** Down to Earth; The Lady From Shanghai. **'48** The Loves of Carmen. **'51** Champagne Safari/Safari So Good (doc). **'52** Affair in Trinidad. **'53** Salome; Miss Sadie Thompson. **'57** Fire Down Below; Pal Joey. **'58** Separate Tables. **'59** They Came to Cordura; The Story on Page One. **'62** The Happy Thieves (GER-SP). **'64** Circus World (GB: The Magnificent Showman). **'65** The Money Trap. **'66** Danger Grows Wild (United Nations) (USA: The Poppy Is Also a Flower). **'67** L'Avventuriero (IT) (USA: The Adventurer; GB: The Rover). **'68** I Bastardi (GER-IT-FR) (USA/GB: Sons of Satan/The Cats). **'70** Sur la Route de Salina (FR-IT) (USA/GB: Road to Salina); The Naked Zoo. **'72** The Wrath of God.

What Katharine Did

More than any other Hollywood heroine, Katharine Hepburn embodied dynamism, courage and idealism. Although compromised by many of her roles, she opened up visions of a fuller life to generations of women

After her bright entry into the firmament of Hollywood in the early Thirties, including an Oscar for Best Actress in *Morning Glory* (1933), Katharine Hepburn's career took a dramatic plunge. Commercial failures such as *Sylvia Scarlett, Mary of Scotland, A Woman Rebels* (all 1936) and *Quality Street* (1937), left her and RKO producer Pandro S. Berman despondent. Despite the overwhelming popularity of *Stage Door* (1937) and the critical acclaim the delightful comedy *Bringing Up Baby* (1938) received, Harry Brandt, President of the Independent Theatre Owners of America, pronounced her 'box-office poison'. Hepburn decided that her career needed a new direction, so she bought herself out of her contract at RKO.

The Forties, despite a 'flat' period in the middle of the decade, were to re-establish her position as a top-rank performer, defining the two major qualities which may be seen as informing both her films and her status as a star – her image as an 'independent' lady and her commitment to left-of-centre politics.

A mind of her own

Her independent image dates back to 1933 and her second film, *Christopher Strong*; the compromises which her roles in this and subsequent films demanded were often wholly subverted by her strong, vivacious personality. *Bringing Up Baby*, however, was the first of her films to show that her headstrong independence could be a major asset in comedy; she and Grant went on to make *Holiday* (1938) and *The Philadelphia Story* (1940), which confirmed her comic talent.

Her next film, *Woman of the Year* (1942), turned out to be crucial both for her career and her private life. It marked the beginning of her long relationship with the picture's co-star,

Spencer Tracy, and was a forerunner of the pair's later and better known comedies on the question of the equality of the sexes, *Adam's Rib* (1949) and *Pat and Mike* (1952).

The meaning of love

These two films, together with *The African Queen* (1951) in which Hepburn starred with Humphrey Bogart, are her most interesting explorations of women's place in society. Not only do they directly confront the issue of the potentialities and role of women as the equals of men and the possibilities for heterosexual relationships under those circumstances, but they do so without unduly compromising their heroines' struggles for self-fulfilment with lame 'male-chauvinist' endings. In addition, *Pat and Mike* and *The African Queen* cast Hepburn as a woman who does not have any advantages of wealth, education or social position – elements which had coloured her earlier roles as an independent woman in films like *Christopher Strong* (1933), *Bringing Up Baby* and *The Philadelphia Story* with a fantastic quality. In *Pat and Mike* Hepburn plays a sportswoman whose confidence is completely destroyed by her fiancé. A small-time sports promoter (Tracy) treats her as an individual and builds up her belief in herself; eventually they fall in love. In *The African Queen*, a rough, alcoholic, Canadian steamer captain (Bogart) finds himself fleeing the Germans with a virgin spinster (Hepburn). Their growing love and respect are intelligently and movingly represented. The film avoids any suggestion that her sexual awakening is a 'gift' bestowed on her by Bogart, but represents each of the protagonists as giving and learning in equal measure.

Hepburn's nine films with Tracy seem to form a central and separate part of her career,

to the point where her other work appears peripheral. After *Woman of the Year* they made *Keeper of the Flame* (1942), in which Hepburn played her first directly political role. As Christine Forrest, the widow of a national figure, she tries to protect her former husband's good name from the investigations of a journalist (Tracy) who correctly suspects him of having been a fascist. The film was aimed at alerting the USA to fascism at home, but sadly it is melodramatic and liberal in the worst sense. Frank Capra's *State of the Union* (1948) was another political film, in which Hepburn helps

Above: Hepburn out walking during the making of The Lion in Winter. *Below: Spencer Tracy looks po-faced as Hepburn turns on the waterworks in* Adam's Rib

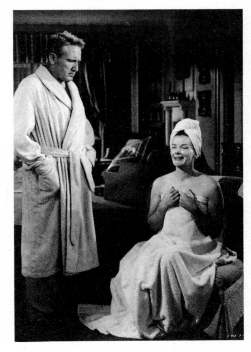

beliefs), many of her roles in the Thirties as an 'independent' heroine were of women from the same moneyed and privileged class. Later on, her roles in *Summer Madness* and *The Rainmaker* could only be seen as conforming to inveterate male attitudes towards female virginity. Her political films suffered not so much from a lack of genuine commitment as from the soft-centredness which liberalism, by definition, produces. On the other hand, given these observations, can she really be criticized for the faults which her films can now be seen to contain? In this regard it is apt to compare her with Jane Fonda, who has had all the advantages of access to contemporary political theory and practice. Today, Fonda's political naivety is both inexcusable and irrelevant, but Hepburn's ingenuousness was not in itself harmful to the positive image she offered – indeed it was part of it. To see Hepburn as she was in the Thirties and Forties is to glimpse not only someone ahead of her time but someone, as David Thomson says in his biographical dictionary, whose 'beauty grew out of her own belief in herself and from the viewer's sense that she was living dangerously, exposing her own nerves and vulnerability along with her intelligence and sensibility.'

That is her triumph, which outweighs all else.   SHEILA WHITAKER

her husband, a presidential candidate (Tracy), recognize that he is being manipulated by crooked politicians.

Rude awakenings

After *Pat and Mike*, Hepburn's career was largely a matter of fine performances in mediocre films. In *Summer Madness* (1955), she plays a repressed spinster who finds love with Rossano Brazzi in Venice; in *The Rainmaker* (1956) she plays Lizzie, another unhappy, small-town spinster who meets Starbuck (Burt Lancaster). In his biography of Hepburn, *Kate*, Charles Higham wrote that Starbuck's:

'. . . physical assurance and powerfully masculine charm break through her protective shell. Starbuck promises to bring rain to the parched soil of the southwestern state, and his promise is metaphorically fulfilled when he enriches Lizzie's sterile and sexless existence.'

Following the disastrous *The Iron Petticoat* (1956), (virtually a remake of Lubitsch's *Ninotchka*, 1939), and the likeable but unremarkable *Desk Set* (1957), which was another permutation on male-female relationships with Tracy, Hepburn was cast in an adaptation of Tennessee Williams' outrageous *Suddenly, Last Summer* (1959). She plays a wealthy widow who tries to hush up the circumstances of her homosexual son's murder by having a pre-frontal lobotomy performed on the only witness, her niece (Elizabeth Taylor). The film is remarkable only for its repressed sense of homosexuality and its representation of a demonic and destructive mother besotted with her dead son, although the film did seem to prompt the confrontation of taboo subjects in later films.

Having given a good performance as the drug-addicted mother in *Long Day's Journey Into Night* (1962), Hepburn made no films for five years in order to nurse an ailing Tracy. Then, in 1967 they made together *Guess Who's Coming to Dinner?*. This was an excruciating, albeit genuinely motivated, liberal 'message' film about the horrors of racial intolerance;

Above: a confrontation between the two redoubtable protagonists of The African Queen, *Hepburn and Humphrey Bogart. Right: George Cukor, who has directed Hepburn in many of her finest performances, the actress herself and Laurence Olivier during the filming of* Love Among the Ruins

Hepburn, however won her second Oscar.

Although she won her third Oscar for her performance in *The Lion in Winter* (1968), her major acting achievement in the Sixties was not on film but on the stage, in the 1960 musical *Coco*, based on the life of Coco Chanel.

In 1975 she played opposite Laurence Olivier in *Love Among the Ruins*, a delightful comedy of lovers meeting again after many years. Directed by George Cukor for American TV, it is a gentle reprise of the theme of male-female relationships explored by her earlier films, and particularly delightful for its portrayal of elderly people rediscovering the excitement of love. Hepburn's next film, *The Corn Is Green* (1978) was also made for TV and directed by Cukor. Sadly, its story of a schoolteacher who helps a young boy miner win a scholarship to Oxford was simplistic and poorly realized.

A free spirit

Apart from her three Oscars, Hepburn was nominated another eight times; she has rightly always been regarded as a vital force in American cinema, although surprisingly little has been written about her. Her extraordinary personality and unconventional private life (not least her wearing of men's clothes) combined with her passionate desire for privacy, particularly during her long affair with Tracy, gave her an aura of freedom. Many of her more successful films capitalized on this image, and for generations of women she offered a vision of life's potential, although with hindsight her career can be seen as entrenched in the ethos of the Hollywood dream factory. Born (in 1909) into a wealthy and privileged upper-middle-class family (although of sound socialist

Filmography
1932 A Bill of Divorcement. '33 Christopher Strong; Morning Glory; Little Women. '34 Spitfire; The Little Minister. '35 Break of Hearts; Alice Adams. '36 Sylvia Scarlett; Mary of Scotland; A Woman Rebels. '37 Quality Street; Stage Door. '38 Bringing Up Baby; Holiday (GB: Free to Live/Unconventional Linda). '40 The Philadelphia Story. '41 Women in Defense (narr. only) (short). '42 Woman of the Year; Keeper of the Flame. '43 Stage Door Canteen. '44 Dragon Seed. '45 Without Love. '46 The Sea of Grass; Undercurrent; The American Creed (guest) (short) (GB: American Brotherhood Week). '47 Song of Love. '48 State of the Union (GB: The World and His Wife). '49 Adam's Rib. '51 The African Queen. '52 Pat and Mike. '55 Summer Madness (USA: Summertime) (USA/GB). '56 The Rainmaker; The Iron Petticoat (GB). '57 Desk Set (GB: His Other Woman). '59 Suddenly, Last Summer. '62 Long Day's Journey Into Night. '67 Guess Who's Coming to Dinner? '68 The Lion in Winter (GB). '69 The Madwoman of Chaillot. '71 The Trojan Women. '73 The Glass Menagerie.* '74 A Delicate Balance.* '75 Rooster Cogburn; Love Among the Ruins.* '78 The Corn Is Green.*
* shot as TV film but shown in cinemas

That Scarlett Woman!

Vivien Leigh's legendary rise to stardom can be traced back to the evening of December 10, 1938, when Atlanta – simulated by a group of old sets – was going up in flames a second time. The long-delayed filming of *Gone With the Wind* (1939) was finally under way, even though the Scarlett O'Hara role remained to be cast – an extraordinary risk for producer David O. Selznick to run. Between setting up the takes, Myron Selznick, one of Hollywood's foremost agents, approached his brother, beckoning from the shadows of the old Pathé back-lot a slender young woman with beautiful eyes. 'Dave,' uttered Myron, for press agents, film fans and raconteurs to quote slavishly for decades to come, 'I want you to meet Scarlett O'Hara.'

That, at least, is the story of how Vivien Leigh came to be cast in the role coveted or claimed at one time or another by every rising, established or waning female star in Hollywood. Perhaps the only exceptions were Barbara Stanwyck (who was aware that her screen persona made her unsuitable for the part) and Hedy Lamarr (whose Viennese accent cancelled her out).

The carefully orchestrated three-year search ended in a *coup de théâtre* with the revelation that an English actress, with only a few films to her credit, was to play the Southern heroine of the novel that, since 1936, had outsold the Bible in the USA. The fact that Vivien Leigh was not American failed to outrage the many

Scarlett O'Hara fan clubs in the Deep South; the unforgivable miscasting would have been to let a Yankee play the role!

After diction lessons, Vivien Leigh successfully added the right touch of molasses to her clipped English delivery. She was also coached (at first officially, later privately) by George Cukor, Selznick's original choice to direct *Gone With the Wind*. She battled constantly with Victor Fleming (the director who replaced Cukor after three weeks), failed to make friends with co-star Clark Gable, threw tantrums on the set and off, and won an Oscar.

The truth about Scarlett?
Her achievement still stands, even if there remains some doubt as to how she came to play the role. Another version of the story is that Victor Saville, the British director who had directed Leigh in *Storm in a Teacup* (1937) rang her London flat one day and said:

'Vivien, I've just read a great story for the movies about the bitchiest of all bitches, and you're just the person to play the part.'

Resolved to try for the part of Scarlett, Leigh

Convent-educated, married at the age of 19 to Ernest Leigh Holman, a man of retiring habits, Vivian Hartley (alias Vivien Leigh) claimed to have little in common with the role of Scarlett O'Hara (top right). But her bewitching blend of innocence, beauty and guile fitted the character like a glove

followed Laurence Olivier – then her paramour, later her husband – to California, where he was to play Heathcliff in Samuel Goldwyn's production of *Wuthering Heights* (1939).

It seems that she was probably seen by – and made a strong impression on – David O. Selznick and Cukor, and was kept under wraps while the continuing search for Scarlett garnered a million dollars' worth of publicity. She was then made to appear, like a rabbit out of Myron Selznick's hat, to snatch the part.

The English rose of Hollywood
At 26 she became a priceless commodity in the industry. David O. Selznick, the sole proprietor of her contract, doled out her talents parsimoniously: first to MGM for *Waterloo Bridge*

(1940), then to Alexander Korda, who had originally discovered Leigh in Britain, for *That Hamilton Woman!* (1941). There followed an absence from the screen dictated by war and sickness. She reappeared as Bernard Shaw's Egyptian kitten of a queen in *Caesar and Cleopatra* (1945), looking ravaged and mature enough to play Shakespeare's Cleopatra.

She was Tennessee Williams' own choice for the part of Blanche DuBois in his play *A Streetcar Named Desire*. The play was filmed in 1951, and this time Leigh's Southern drawl was so convincing that it seemed to issue from a dark, bruised recess of her being. A sense of inevitable decline is captured in the curtain line: 'After all, I've always depended on the kindness of strangers' – a melancholy echo of that other famous exit line: 'After all, tomorrow is another day', which summed up the headstrong, vixenish, egotistical Scarlett.

Living close to the edge

Various screen tests for Scarlett have survived and been screened: Leigh's has disappeared into some clandestine collection, but we have Cukor's word that no-one, not even Leigh herself during the actual shooting of the film, could match her miraculously intuitive approach on that first brush with the part.

Bottom: Alexander Korda capitalized on Leigh and Olivier's much-publicized affair by casting them as Lady Hamilton and Lord Nelson in That Hamilton Woman! *Above right: severe bouts of depression marred her performance as Anna Karenina which failed to match Garbo's earlier portrayal. Centre right: Leigh as the Egyptian queen in* Caesar and Cleopatra. *Bottom right: Blanche in* A Streetcar Named Desire, *clinging to her fading beauty and her dreams of romance in a brutal world, was her last great screen appearance. The film's sexual frankness caused a storm of controversy*

Around her Scarlett one perceives, even now, not just the whims and caprices of a spoiled beauty, but real hovering demons; the same which would overwhelm her later in her private life. As early as *Fire Over England* (1937), she seemed a needlessly neurotic lady-in-waiting, but while she was young such traits could be taken as eccentricities. Watching Vivien Leigh glow in inferior pictures like *The Roman Spring of Mrs Stone* (1961) or *Ship of Fools* (1965), there is the strong impression of a trained performer drawing perilously close to lived experience; in *The Deep Blue Sea* (1955), she is almost too genuine for comfort playing a woman caught between suicide attempts.

Vivien Leigh's own life had been one of extremes. Born in 1913 in India, separated in childhood from her mother, she struggled with bouts of hysteria and depression before contracting tuberculosis in 1945. She fought the disease throughout her life until finally succumbing to it in 1967. But these bare facts do not explain her peculiar 'poetic' nervousness.

Tennessee Williams celebrated a certain breed of women as 'ladies who died when love was lost'. This definition, though it misses Scarlett, encompasses Blanche, Anna Karenina, Mrs Stone and Mrs Mary Treadwell of *Ship of Fools*, and may stand as a fitting, if melancholy, epitaph for Vivian Leigh herself.

CARLOS CLARENS

Filmography

1935 Things Are Looking Up; The Village Squire; Gentleman's Agreement; Look Up and Laugh. **'37** Fire Over England; Dark Journey (cut version issued as The Anxious Years); Storm in a Teacup; (USA; 21 Days Together). **'38** A Yank at Oxford. **'39** St Martin's Lane (USA: Sidewalks of London); Gone With the Wind (USA). **'40** Waterloo Bridge (USA). **'41** That Hamilton Woman! (GB: Lady Hamilton) (USA). **'45** Caesar and Cleopatra. **'48** Anna Karenina. **'51** A Streetcar Named Desire (USA). **'55** The Deep Blue Sea. **'61** The Roman Spring of Mrs Stone (USA). **'65** Ship of Fools (USA).

Carole Lombard
the Glamorous Madcap

She was beautiful, but it is not her beauty we remember; it is her wit and intelligence. She had Eve Arden's sharp tongue, the good-natured toughness of Ginger Rogers and the elegant zaniness of Lucille Ball, combined with a tender vulnerability all her own. Her side-long sexuality and offhand comedy make most of today's actresses look old-fashioned. She played it 'cool' before 'cool' was invented

Born into one of the 'better' families of Fort Wayne, Indiana on October 6, 1908, Carole Lombard, the queen of screwball comedy, was discovered – during a visit to friends – by the director Allan Dwan. Then called Jane Peters, she was playing baseball in the street with her brothers. Dwan gave her the part of a tomboy in his film *A Perfect Crime* (1921).

Between 1929 and 1942, when she was tragically killed in an air crash, she made around forty films of varying quality. In 1927 (after a short spell at Fox) Lombard spent a year with Mack Sennett, and although his days of glory were almost over he helped to build the foundations of her comedy technique. This, when added to her generous output, goes some way to explain how she was able to refine her performance to the brilliance of her greatest comedies: *Twentieth Century* (1934), *My Man Godfrey* (1936), *Nothing Sacred* (1937) and *To Be or Not to Be* (1942).

Despite her careering energy Lombard always remained in control. She never indulged herself or the character she was playing. In *No Man of Her Own* (1932), with Clark Gable (who was to become her second husband in 1939), her steadfast refusal to give in to the maudlin romanticism of the piece gives the film whatever redeeming bite it still possesses. In *Hands Across the Table* (1935) she worked with Mitchell Leisen, next to Lubitsch the director whose elegance most closely matched her own. He was the antithesis of Howard Hawks who directed her in *Twentieth Century* and was always a touch crude (despite his manifest virtues), forcing the pace, not allowing his women time to breathe; and he treated his actors and actresses in exactly the same way. Leisen admirably kept the balance between romance and light comedy – and for once the comedy is truly light. Lombard's playing is here at its most delicate as a manicurist coping with the boring attentions of the crippled millionaire Ralph Bellamy, only to fall for the shifty charm of Fred MacMurray. Her scenes with MacMurray are as sharp as the instrument with which she nervously shreds his fingernails.

slightly theatrical performance and Ben Hecht's script – which starts with a brilliant idea but then does not have the courage to exploit its full bad-taste potential.

No such inhibitions mask *To Be or Not to Be*, her most stylishly intelligent film and therefore her best. This great comedy chronicles the exploits, in Nazi-occupied Poland, of a group of ham actors. As the Gestapo chief remarks about the leader of the troupe: 'He did to Shakespeare what we are doing to Poland.' Lombard's performance remains central to the success of this masterpiece.

Lombard's first entrance sets the tone. The troupe is rehearsing a play set in Nazi Germany. Lombard (playing Maria Tura) enters in a stunning evening gown. The director stops the rehearsal to point out that the scene is actually set in a German concentration camp and how could she exhibit such appalling taste? Her look of petulance at such irritating objections says everything about her incessant

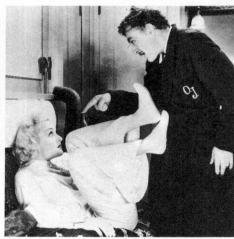

Lombard could embody a character and criticize it too. She treated herself with the same wry detachment. Though the phrase 'Brechtian actress' conjures up the gaunt earnestness of a Helen Weigel, the very opposite of the stylish Carole Lombard, yet Brecht would have admired her speed, lightness and objectivity.

When actresses play actresses, they usually fall into the trap of being bitchy yet lovable. Even the great Bette Davis was guilty of not being as ruthless with herself as she was with others in *All About Eve* (1950). Lombard, in *Twentieth Century* and *To Be or Not to Be*, exposes the necessary heartlessness of the profession which is all heart. Her actresses are beautiful and lethal, with a remorseless egotism concealed behind a blissful charm. They have to be, of course, for they are in competition with such unrepentant monomaniacs as Jack Benny and John Barrymore.

By not playing cute she becomes endearing, and by not asking to be liked she is effortlessly likeable – never more so than when she acted opposite her first husband William Powell (they divorced in 1933) in *My Man Godfrey*, perhaps the most famous screwball comedy of the American Depression. As the scatter-brained daughter of an idle-rich family scavenger-hunting for an authentic derelict and 'forgotten man' (a Depression term for down-and-out), Lombard makes us forget the distasteful nature of the film and its ambivalent social stance.

There is not a whiff of sentimentality in her portrait of Hazel Flagg, the working girl supposedly dying of radium poisoning in *Nothing Sacred*, who is slobbered over by the New York press and public. Her scenes with her testy doctor Charles Winninger – who is more concerned that he was once cheated by a New

York newspaper competition than by her medical condition – are delicate pieces of black comedy. Her initial response to the news of her illness is piercingly true, being a combination of disbelief, horror, and a self-dramatizing pride in the fact that she has been picked out to be struck down.

Women drunks are rarely funny or elegant. Lombard is both in *Nothing Sacred*, when she attacks March in a drunken fury. She shows true grace under pressure, particularly under the pressures of William Wellman's straight-up-and-down direction, Fredric March's

Above left: Lombard, then still married to William Powell, in No Man of Her Own *(1932), her only picture with Gable. Above: with John Barrymore in* Twentieth Century *(1934). Below: as a fan-dancer on the make in* Lady by Choice *(1934)*

just one more backdrop to display her histrionic talents. Yet she never loses our sympathy because she is always human. When the troupe finally parachutes into England and the press ask her husband what he wants to do, Lombard answers for him: 'He wants to play Hamlet,' she says with a tender weariness that is unexpectedly touching.

In *To Be or Not to Be*, Lombard shows, in the face of the brutality and unimagined stupidity of men in power, that one should not lose one's style. Lose everything else, but with style despair can be kept at bay. With Carole Lombard, courage has a tiny smile; the hidden emotions come elegantly draped in a Paris gown. Above this, she had a quality, as rare in films as it is in life: she had class.

PETER BARNES

Above: divorced in private life but teamed on the screen, Lombard and Powell in My Man Godfrey *(1936), one of the brightest comedies of the decade. Above right: a more romantic comedy followed in 1937,* Swing High, Swing Low, *with Lombard playing an entertainer who uses – but falls in love with – a trumpeter, Fred MacMurray. Below: in* Hands Across the Table *(1935), Lombard and MacMurray also play cynical roles, but love continues to conquer all. Right: Lombard in* To Be or Not to Be *(1942), shortly before her death in an air crash during a government-bond selling tour*

role-playing and refusal to concede to the grubby requirements of naturalism.

Her performance – good taste in bad taste – is a consummate display of tiny expressive visual gestures learnt in silent movies and a mocking verbal delivery at all-out speed. Whether flattering a German spy ('I am honoured – and *thrilled*.'), encouraging the attentions of a handsome flyer or dealing with her husband's non-sleeping paranoia, she is always conscious, in her eyes at least, that she is a great actress and that devastated Europe is

Filmography
1921 A Perfect Crime. '25 Gold and the Girl; Marriage in Transit; Hearts and Spurs; Durand of the Badlands. '27 The Fighting Eagle; Smith's Pony (short); A Gold Digger of Weepah (short); The Girl From Everywhere (short). '28 Run, Girl, Run (short); The Beach Club (short); The Best Man (short); The Swim Princess (short); The Bicycle Flirt (short); The Divine Sinner; The Girl From Nowhere (short); His Unlucky Night (short); The Campus Vamp (short); Power; Me, Gangster; Show Folks; The Campus Carmen (short); Ned McCobb's Daughter. '29 Matchmaking Venus/Matchmaking Mamas (short); High Voltage (GB: Wanted); Big News. '30 The Racketeer (GB: Love's Conquest); The Arizona Kid; Safety in Numbers; Fast and Loose. '31 It Pays to Advertise; Man of the Wild; Ladies' Man; Up Pops the Devil; Take This Woman. '32 No One Man; Sinners in the Sun; Virtue; No More Orchids; No Man of Her Own. '33 From Hell to Heaven; Supernatural; The Eagle and the Hawk; Brief Moment; White Woman. '34 Bolero; We're Not Dressing; Twentieth Century; Now and Forever; Lady by Choice; The Gay Bride. '35 Rumba; Hands Across the Table. '36 Love Before Breakfast; The Princess Comes Across; My Man Godfrey. '37 Swing High, Swing Low; Nothing Sacred; True Confession. '38 Fools for Scandal. '39 Made for Each Other; In Name Only. '40 Vigil in the Night; Picture People No 4 (short); They Knew What They Wanted. '41 Mr and Mrs Smith. '42 To Be or Not to Be.

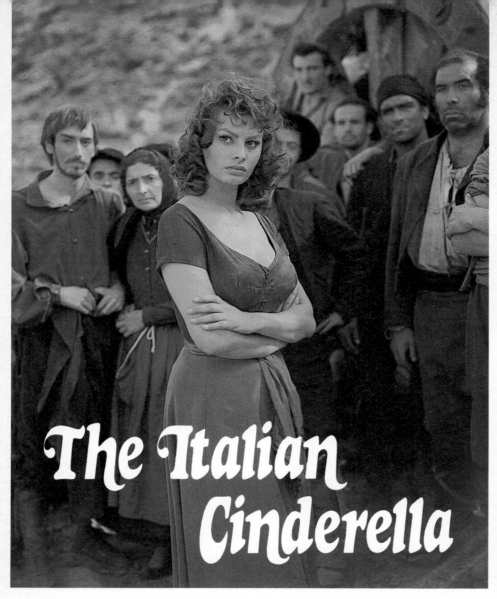

The Italian Cinderella

The real-life fairy story of Sophia Loren: from poverty in a war-torn Italian village, to the luxury of life as one of the world's most admired, individual and stunningly beautiful actresses

'Sophia is perhaps the only movie star who has never forgotten where she came from', a close acquaintance of the actress once observed – and in a profession where origins are often deliberately obscured or fabricated by publicists for popular consumption the details of Loren's early background do carry a rare stamp of truth. It is a background that has always informed her best work, be it in her lusty Neapolitan comedies or dramas set in the war-racked years when Southern Italy bore the brunt of bombings, famine and disease. Loren was, moreover, illegitimate and it is to her mother's eternal credit that she refused to place her daughter in an orphanage but prefered to face the ignominy and disgrace that would inevitably be their lot in the intensely moral, small town of Pozzuoli where they lived. The father, however, did consent to give the child his name and thus she was christened Sofia Scicolone. The year was 1934.

During the war, when the tide of fortune began to turn in the Allies' favour, the bombings became more and more persistent and after the last train to Naples had passed through, the inhabitants of Pozzuoli repaired nightly to a stinking tunnel where, starving and riddled with particularly virulent lice, they would remain until the first morning train was signalled. And when living in Naples the young Sofia and her mother witnessed the most horrendous atrocities as the street urchins banded together to harass the Germans, often sacrificing themselves in order to set fire to German tanks and trucks.

Curtain calls

Sofia's mother always had a fierce determination that her daughter should make her own way in life, and this probably stemmed from an early bitter disappointment of her own, when she had won a competition for the closest resemblance to Garbo. The prize was a trip to Hollywood and a screen test at MGM, but her parents had refused to let her go, owing to the prevalent Italian rumour that Valentino had been murdered by the New York Mafia – a fate that, in their eyes, must await all Italians bent on a Hollywood career. Sofia was a skinny child who had always been referred to derisively by her schoolmates as 'The Toothpick', but at the age of 14 she began to blossom and

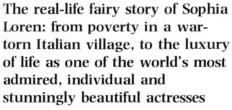

Far left: Loren as first seen by a wider international audience in The Pride and the Passion, *which co-starred Cary Grant. Bottom left: a publicity shot from their next film together,* Houseboat. *Left: Loren gave an Oscar-winning performance in* Two Women,

directed by Vittorio De Sica. Above left: she acted with De Sica in La Bella Mugnaia *(1955,* The Miller's Wife*). Above: Loren with husband, the producer Carlo Ponti; after* Heller in Pink Tights *(right) failed they left Hollywood for Italy and superior roles*

her mother entered her in a Naples beauty contest which she won in a dress improvised from the living-room curtains. The prize was a mixed bag of blessings: a railway ticket to Rome, a table cloth with matching napkins, some rolls of wallpaper and about thirty-five dollars.

Their first introduction to a film studio came when Sofia heard a rumour that hundreds of extras were needed for a film in Rome. This was enough for the mother to pack their bags and they both secured four days' crowd work in director Mervyn LeRoy's *Quo Vadis* (1951). But no more work was forthcoming. Moreover, they received news that Sofia's young sister – a second illegitimate child by the same father (who this time had refused to give the child his name) – was ill in Pozzuoli. Sofia was left alone in Rome in the reluctant charge of some distant cousins. She found work being photographed for the popular cheapjack newspaper serial stories – *fumetti* – and it was not until she entered another beauty contest, in which she was placed second, that she came close to the cinema again, for the jury was composed entirely of movie people.

Her pride and passion

One in particular favoured her – his name was Carlo Ponti. During the course of the next year, Ponti arranged several screen tests for Sofia whose name had now been changed by the *fumetti* producer to Sofia Lazzaro. All the tests were negative and the cameramen's complaints all the same: her mouth was too wide, her nose too long, her hips too wide – a far cry from the modish film star's face of the period. In despair Ponti suggested that she have a nose operation, but she declared, in an unusual burst of self-confidence for her at the time, that she preferred to stay as she was.

Back in Rome, Sofia's mother was tireless in her search for work for her daughter and the result was a series of unremarkable bit parts during the course of which a producer decided

to change her name yet again to Sophia Loren. Her first leading role was *Aida* (1953), mouthing the words to the voice of the reigning operatic star, Renata Tebaldi. The million lire that she earned from this sufficed to buy her father's permission for his second daughter to assume his name legally. At this point, Sophia met the second great influence on her professional life, Vittorio De Sica.

De Sica did not forget their encounter and eventually offered her a part in one of the six episodes in *L'Oro di Napoli* (1954, *The Gold of Naples*). In this fellow-Neapolitan Loren found a director whom she could trust; their understanding was instinctual and immediate and she was able to release her emotions as never before, secure in the knowledge that he would dexterously control her performance. As the wife of a pasta vendor Loren made a hit, not only in Italy but abroad. During that year and the next she was to appear in four films with De Sica as an actor and was also to act with Marcello Mastroianni; thus the Neapolitan trio, who were to work so often together in the future, was forged.

Loren was by now under exclusive contract to Ponti who was already aiming to place her in American movies. In between takes and at every available moment she was subjected to a crash course in English. Before she was really at ease with the language he had secured her the leading role in director Stanley Kramer's *The Pride and the Passion* (1957) with Cary Grant and Frank Sinatra.

Lost in Hollywood

Hollywood has a blemished record in dealing with Italian actresses. Even the great Anna Magnani, despite winning an Oscar for *The Rose Tattoo* (1955), failed to find subsequent material to match her earthy, explosive talent and soon returned to Italy. Loren fared little better; and the remarkably wide range of material in which she played seems to indicate that no-one – not even Ponti – knew quite

what to do with her. Early on, she appeared in *Legend of the Lost* (1957), a rubbishy piece with John Wayne about the discovery in the desert of an archaeological treasure, and she was also saddled with director Delbert Mann's artificially lit, studio-bound production of Eugene O'Neill's play *Desire Under the Elms* (1958), cast opposite that most introspective of actors, Anthony Perkins. Two films during this period came near to revealing a relaxed, jokey Loren: *Houseboat* (1958) with Cary Grant (the actress's strong personal attachment to Grant must have lent her confidence), and a bizarre Western, *Heller in Pink Tights* (1960), directed by George Cukor, whose imaginative flair for bringing out the best in his leading ladies from Judy Holliday to Hepburn and Garbo, is legendary. But Loren did not appeal to a large public as a blonde-bewigged leading lady in a group of travelling players who gambles her virtue in a game with a killer. The actress seemed to have lost her way. In England she fared only marginally better, playing the world's richest woman, opposite Peter Sellers as the doctor who eludes her advances, in *The Millionairess* (1960). The film was based on George Bernard Shaw's play but her performance and Anthony Asquith's direction lacked the necessary panache to allow Shaw's dialogue to sparkle. She needed to return to Italy and De Sica to discover her full potential.

Move over Magnani

La Ciociara (1961, *Two Women*) was originally intended as a vehicle for Magnani. Alberto Moravia's story of a mother and her daughter in war-time Italy who, while making their way back to their native village, are raped by marauding Moroccan troups, was set in an emotional climate that Loren vividly remembered.

Magnani was to play the mother and Loren the daughter but Magnani obstinately refused this casting. Finally the roles were adapted for Loren to play the mother with a much younger daughter. Under De Sica's perceptive direction she rose superbly to the challenge. She had now become mature enough as an actress to draw inspiration from her early memories and re-create them with exceptional artistic strength. She had learnt to act with her whole being and when she was awarded the Oscar for her performance – the first time it was ever given for a performance in a foreign-language film – it must have seemed like a vindication for the predominantly second-rate material she had been offered in her American productions.

The next 13 years showed Loren in more misses than hits. On the credit side were: *El Cid* (1961), which saw Loren, under Anthony Mann's direction, sandwiched between a spectacular single-handed combat and a final impressive battle; *Le Couteau dans la Plaie* (1962, *Five Miles to Midnight*), a modest thriller

in which she was well cast, for once, as the Italian wife of an American in Paris: and *Arabesque* (1966), which saw her give a delightful performance as an oil magnate's mistress opposite Gregory Peck as a linguistics expert. Ponti was also wise enough to bring Loren back to her native scene in two films by De Sica, *Ieri, Oggi e Domani* (1964, *Yesterday, Today and Tomorrow*) and *Matrimonio all'Italiana* (1964, *Marriage Italian Style*). In both films she was reunited with Marcello Mastroianni and although some British critics found the films too salacious and brash for comfort the director and his stars marvellously evoked the spirit and rhythm of the raffish, warm and defiant Naples they all knew so well.

On the debit side were such dead losses as Anthony Mann's *The Fall of the Roman Empire* (1964), Daniel Mann's *Judith* (1965) with its stilted script by Lawrence Durrell, and the screen version of the American musical success, *Man of La Mancha* (1972) with Peter O'Toole, misguidedly shot in the Rome studios instead of the Spanish countryside. There was also the fiasco of the last Chaplin venture, *A Countess From Hong Kong* (1967) in which the actress starred with a Brando who acted as if he wished he were miles away.

A special role

It was not until 1977 that Loren found a vehicle that fully revealed once again her characteristic warmth and humanity which not even the appallingly dubbed version

Above right: Loren in I Girasoli *(1970, Sunflower). Right: with Michel Albertini in* Verdict *(1974). Below right: a production shot from* A Special Day *with Marcello Mastroianni. Below: with a moody Marlon Brando in* A Countess From Hong Kong

Above: some reflected glory in Arabesque *in which Loren plays the exotic mistress of a fetishistic Arab oil magnate (Alan Badel). Left: Marcello Mastroianni and Sophia relax during the making of* La Moglie del Prete *(1970, The Priest's Wife)*

shown in England could subdue. Director-screenwriter Ettore Scola's *Una Giornata Particolare (A Special Day)*, shot in muted tones which perfectly evoked its World War II setting, presented Loren as a mother of six children who chances to meet an outcast homosexual, played by Mastroianni, in a deserted block of flats whose inhabitants are all attending a monster rally in celebration of Hitler's visit to Mussolini's Rome. Their brief encounter and subsequent inevitable separation was beautifully, bleakly traced with never

a false emphasis.

Was it out of a desire to counter the incessant calumnies to which the Ponti-Loren ménage has been constantly submitted through the years (particularly by the Italian press and the Vatican which, for some years branded him as a bigamist and her as his concubine, refusing to accept his Mexican divorce as legal) that they decided to make a $3 million television version of her life based on the book *Sophia: Living and Loving* which she wrote with A. E. Hotchner? Perhaps; but the project presented a big producer's problem: was it wise to keep your superstar waiting in the wings while three other actresses portray her early years until she herself takes over at the age of 23? The solution was beautiful in its simplicity: Loren also plays her own mother.

DEREK PROUSE

Filmography

Films as Sofia Scicolone unless otherwise specified: **1950** Cuori sul Mare (IT-FR); Le Sei Mogli di Barbablù. **'51** Quo Vadis (extra) (USA); Era Lui, Sì, Sì (as Sofia Lazzaro); Io Sono il Capataz; Milano Miliardaria; Il Voto. **'52** E'Arrivato l'Accordatore (as Sofia Lazzaro); Anna (as Sofia Lazzaro); Mago per Forza; Il Sogno di Zorro. *All remaining films as Sophia Loren:* **'52** La Tratta delle Bianche (USA/GB: Girls Marked for Danger reissued as The White Slave Trade). **'53** Africa Sotto i Mari; Aida; Ci Troviamo in Galleria; Due Notti con Cleopatra; La Favorita. **'54** Carosello Napoletano (USA: Neapolitan Carousel; GB: Neapolitan Fantasy); La Domenica della Buona Gente; Un Giorno in Pretura (USA: A Day in Court); Miseria e Nobiltà; L'Oro di Napoli *ep* Pizze e Credito (USA: Gold of Naples; GB: Every Day's a Holiday/Gold of Naples); Il Paese dei Campanelli (IT-FR); Tempi Nostri *ep* La Macchina Fotografica) (USA: Anatomy of Love; GB: A Slice of Life). **'55** Attila Flagello di Dio (IT-FR) (USA: Attila; GB: Attila the Hun); La Bella Mugnaia (USA: The Miller's Beautiful Wife; GB: The Miller's Wife); La Donna del Fiume (IT-FR) (USA/GB: Woman of the River); Pane, Amore e . . . (USA/GB: Scandal in Sorrento); Peccato che Sia una Canaglia (USA/GB: Too Bad She's Bad); Pellegrini d'Amore; Il Segno di Venere (GB: The Sign of Venus). **'56** La Fortuna di Essere Donna (IT-FR) (USA/GB: Lucky to be a Woman). **'57** The Pride and the Passion (USA); Boy on a Dolphin (USA); Legend of the Lost (USA-PAN-IT). **'58** Desire Under the Elms (USA); Houseboat (USA); The Key (GB); The Black Orchid (USA). **'59** That Kind of Woman (USA). **'60** Heller in Pink Tights (USA); A Breath of Scandal/Olympia (USA-IT-A); It Started in Naples (USA); The Millionairess (GB). **'61** La Ciociara (IT-FR) (USA/GB: Two Women); El Cid (USA-IT). **'62** Boccaccio '70 *ep* The Raffle (IT-FR); Madame Sans-Gene (IT-FR-SP) (USA: Madame); I Sequestrati di Altona (IT-FR) (USA/GB: The Condemned of Altona); Le Couteau dans la Plaie (FR-IT) (USA/GB: Five Miles to Midnight). **'64** Ieri, Oggi e Domani (IT) (USA/GB: Yesterday, Today and Tomorrow); The Fall of the Roman Empire (USA-IT); Matrimonio all'Italiana (IT-FR) (USA/GB: Marriage Italian Style). **'65** Operation Crossbow (GB-IT); Lady L (FR-IT); Judith (USA-IS). **'66** Arabesque (USA-GB). **'67** A Countess From Hong Kong (GB); C'Era una Volta (IT-FR) (USA: More Than a Miracle/Once Upon a Time/Happily Ever After; GB: Cinderella – Italian Style). **'68** Questi Fantasmi (IT-FR) (USA/GB: Ghosts, Italian Style). **'70** I Girasoli (IT-USSR) (USA/GB: Sunflower); La Moglie del Prete (IT-FR) (USA/GB: The Priest's Wife). **'71** La Mortadella (IT-FR) (USA: Lady Liberty); Bianco, Rosso e . . . (IT-FR-SP) (USA: White Sister/The Sin). **'72** Man of La Mancha. **'74** Il Viaggio (IT) (USA/GB: The Voyage/The Journey); Verdict (FR-IT); La Pupa del Gangster (IT-FR). **'77** The Cassandra Crossing (GB-IT-GER); Una Giornata Particolare (IT-CAN) (USA/GB: A Special Day); Angela (CAN). **'78** Brass Target (USA). **'79** Fatto di Sangue Fra Due Uomini (IT) (USA/GB: Blood Feud); Firepower (GB).

The Blonde Gentlemen Prefer

The trials and tribulations and the incendiary mixture of wide-eyed innocence and sumptuous sexiness have often obscured the fact that Marilyn Monroe was a supreme talent, 'as near genius as any actress I ever knew' said Joshua Logan who directed her in *Bus Stop*. There was certainly no-one else like her . . .

Hollywood's great stars seldom seem to have been the products of happy homes and stable childhoods. Chaplin's father walked out on the family when his son was one year old, and Fairbanks' when Douglas was four. Mary Pickford's father died when she was four, Valentino's when he was eleven, Garbo's when she was thirteen. Marilyn Monroe was never even certain who her father was: he may have been a mechanic called Mortensen or a film-laboratory employee called Gifford, or a Mr Baker who was the father of her elder brother and sister. For safety's sake, early publicity gave it out that whoever he was he had been killed in a car crash shortly after the birth of his daughter.

Like Chaplin again, Marilyn was committed to an orphanage after her mother retreated into madness. In her case the legacy of mental instability was more terrifying: her maternal grandfather and grandmother – a fanatical disciple of the evangelist Aimee Semple Mac-Pherson, in whose temple Marilyn was baptised Norma Jeane Mortensen – ended their lives in mental institutions.

Unlike the other great stars, however, Norma Jean (the final 'e' only appears on her birth certificate) was a child of the movie capital. She was born, on June 1, 1926, in the Los Angeles General Hospital. Her room in the Los Angeles Orphan home is said to have looked directly onto the neon sign over RKO studios, and Marilyn later told interviewers that one of the most wonderful memories of her childhood was a Christmas party given by RKO for the orphan children, when she was nine. None of her biographies or interviews reveal at what age this apparently lonely, shy and introverted girl conceived the determination to become a movie star; but that determination must have been single-minded and steely to survive the inevitable years of disappointment and frustration that she was to experience after her first arrival at 20th Century-Fox.

At the time World War II ended she was working in an aircraft factory, testing parachutes, when a photographer taking official propaganda pictures spotted her potential and introduced her to an agent, Emmeline Snively. By 1946 she was launched as a pin-up and cover girl, and a smart publicity stunt secured a test at Fox. Ben Lyon, the actor, who was then the studio's talent scout, advised her to change her name: Monroe was her grandmother's married name; Marilyn was Lyon's suggestion – a tribute to an earlier star, Marilyn Miller. She was signed by Fox for a year and went through the familiar processing of potential starlets: she was photographed; given

a couple of small parts – one of which, in *Scudda Hoo! Scudda Hay!* (1948) was entirely cut out – but the studio did not renew her contract.

By this time, however, Marilyn seems already to have been actively organizing her career. She kept up her classes at the Actors'

Laboratory where she had been enrolled by Fox; acquired the first of the personal drama coaches who were later to try the patience of her directors; and made good use of the admirers, advisers, patrons and protectors – the most significant of them was the agent Johnny Hyde, thirty years her senior – whom she readily attracted. She won a featured role in a Columbia musical, *Ladies of the Chorus* (1948), was chased by Groucho Marx in *Love Happy* (1949), and received her first small but favourable critical attention for the role of a crooked lawyer's girl in *The Asphalt Jungle* (1950). Its director John Huston – who some 11 years later was to guide her patiently and painfully through her last completed film, *The Misfits* (1961) – told her, 'You know, Marilyn, you're going to be a good actress'.

She had already had half a dozen small parts when she walked through *All About Eve*

had advised the film business, 'Don't fool yourself. This girl is a coming star'. Much later, on Laurence Olivier's *The Prince and the Show-girl* (1957), there appears to have been a touching mutual admiration and affection between Marilyn and the veteran Dame Sybil Thorndike.

The three years between *Niagara* and *Bus Stop* (1956) were the peak of her professional career, a period comparatively untroubled by the personal problems that were eventually to dog her. A keen judge of material – her intelligent rejection of scripts often caused friction with the studio – she regretted Otto Preminger's *River of No Return* (1954) as a miscalculation, a crude exploitation of her sexual attractions.

It is almost inconceivable now that so many of Marilyn's contemporaries were sceptical about her technical achievements and about her ambitions to be a serious artist – her touchingly demanding literary pursuits and her work with Lee and Paula Strasberg at the Actors' Studio in New York. Her performances in *Gentlemen Prefer Blondes* and *How to Marry a Millionaire* show a refined and precious comic talent; in the latter she plays an acutely myopic beauty forever crashing into walls when, from vanity, she discards her enormous spectacles. In *There's No Business Like Show Business* (1954), developing her endearing, funny, baby singing voice, she parodies the conventions of the stage musical star. In *The Seven Year Itch* (1955) she proves an altogether equal comedy partner to old hand Tom Ewell and outstrips the director Billy Wilder with the subtlety of her comic effects. The climax of this period of her career, however, is reached in Joshua

Above left: Marilyn Monroe – 'a beautiful profile all the way down' – with Yves Montand (in tails) in Let's Make Love. *Top: Marilyn's look and Groucho's leer in* Love Happy. *Above and below: dramatic roles in* The Asphalt Jungle *and* Don't Bother to Knock. *Right: as Lorelei Lee in* Gentlemen Prefer Blondes, *with Jane Russell*

(1950), leaving behind one of the first authentic 'Monroisms'. As Miss Caswell, a starlet, she arrives at a party on the arm of stage critic Addison DeWitt (George Sanders) who suavely introduces her to Margo Channing (Bette Davis), 'You know Miss Caswell, of course?' 'No', Margo mercilessly snaps back. 'That', smiles Miss Caswell guilelessly, 'is because we

never met.' Marilyn became well known for such deceptively artless and worryingly enigmatic ripostes.

The public had already noticed her, and her parts became bigger and more significant. In 1952 Fox made the mistake of casting her in a dramatic role – as a psychopathic girl in *Don't Bother to Knock*. The notices and the box-office returns were bad, but in retrospect it is a creditable performance, with moments of intuition and intensity which may well have been stirred by the parallels to her own childhood.

The three Marilyn Monroe films that were released in 1953 – *Niagara*, *Gentlemen Prefer Blondes* and *How to Marry a Millionaire* – definitively established her as a star and a new sex image for the age. *Niagara*, Henry Hathaway's tongue-in-cheek handling of a torrid melodrama of passion, teamed Marilyn's own natural splendours with the Niagara falls – and introduced 'The Walk' with a 70-foot shot of Marilyn undulating away from the camera in uncomfortable high heels across cobble-stones. Her unique ambulation was a celebration of her sensuous physique, a positive percussion and choreography of limbs, buttocks and the thighs that seem to have an extra curve (she always gave out her *upper* and *lower* hip measurement). In *Gentlemen Prefer Blondes* she was teamed with Jane Russell, and in *How to Marry a Millionaire* with Betty Grable and Lauren Bacall. It was no doubt Monroe's presence that made both films major box-office hits; but she always seemed to work well with other actresses of character and intelligence and to inspire their liking. Working with her on *Clash by Night* (1952), Barbara Stanwyck

Above: Marilyn as a saloon singer in River of No Return. *Right: as gold-digger Pola with Mr Denmark (David Wayne) disproving that men never make passes at girls who wear glasses in* How to Marry a Millionaire

Logan's *Bus Stop*, with a comic performance of flair and charm and pathos that transcends the stage-bound screenplay.

Already Marilyn was regarded as a 'difficult' actress. Her attendances on the set became more and more erratic. For a while she abandoned Hollywood for New York and her mentor, Lee Strasberg. At this time too she acquired Paula Strasberg, his wife, as a new

---

'I want to be an artist . . . not an erotic freak. I don't want to be sold to the public as a celluloid aphrodisiacal'

---

drama coach to replace Natasha Lytess. First married at 16, Marilyn later became the wife of the baseball star Joe Di Maggio in 1954, but the marriage foundered after a year. A third marriage to the playwright Arthur Miller and her appearance alongside Olivier in *The Prince and the Showgirl*, her only British film, seemed the culmination of her cultural ambitions.

Her private life had begun to darken, however. Already there was the horrifying dependence on drugs, and prolonged periods in mental clinics. The unpunctuality and absenteeism which had first seemed a caprice were revealed as symptoms of sickness. She

became hard to work with. She is charming and funny in Billy Wilder's *Some Like It Hot* (1959), but her co-star Tony Curtis said, 'Kissing Marilyn Monroe was like kissing Hitler'. Curtis wears women's clothing for most of the film and Marilyn serenely retorted to his ungallant remark, 'He only said that because I had prettier dresses than he did'.

Let's Make Love (1960) was the most insignificant film of her later career, despite George Cukor's direction and the lift to her morale provided by her affair with co-star Yves Montand. Finally she struggled through *The Misfits*. Her marriage to Arthur Miller – who

had scripted the film and had clearly based the character of Roslyn on his wife – was breaking up. She was sick, frequently quite incapacitated by narcotics, and repeatedly hospitalized. Still Marilyn's performance is one of the finest of her career: she seemed only to gain in depth and insight. Some of her most touching scenes are those when Roslyn expresses her horror at the inhumanity of the men to the mustangs they are catching: Marilyn always revealed an extreme and even neurotic empathy with animals and children.

She began work, again with Cukor, on *Something's Got to Give* in 1962. But she

appeared on the set only 12 times in the first month of shooting. Fox fired her and sued for compensation. Seven weeks later, on August

'Talent is developed in privacy . . . but everybody is always tugging at you. They'd all like sort of a chunk of you. They'd kind of like to take pieces out of you'

5, she died from a drug overdose. She was 36. The few brief sequences that she had shot for *Something's Got to Give* showed a new and metamorphosed Marilyn. There was little trace of the round-faced pin-up of the early days in this woman of breathtaking grace, beauty, luminosity and awful fragility. In a series of costume tests she walks and walks again (and by this time she no longer undulates, but floats); and the hieratic, ritual magic of the rushes is haunting and unforgettable.

Marilyn belonged to the last years of the studio system and the last real generation of stars. Her contemporaries included Grace Kelly, Audrey Hepburn, Marlon Brando, James Dean, Kim Novak and the grown-up Elizabeth Taylor. She hated being a sex symbol ('I thought symbols were something you clash'); yet she was one of the most potent embodiments of sexuality the screen has ever known. It seemed to emanate from her own exultation and fascination with her physique and sexuality. 'I'm very certainly a woman and I enjoy it,' she said. She was said to wear her dresses two sizes too small so that she was always conscious, from their clinging, of every part of her body. She liked to look at herself in mirrors. When she moves or stands or sits, she gives the impression that she is unconsciously feeling and testing and *enjoying* every limb and nerve. The nude bathing scene filmed for *Something's Got to Give* survives, an act of solitary devotion.

With the sexuality, however, there went a refined comic technique. We can never know to what extent it was instinctive and to what extent developed by her very intense and serious studies in the studios and with her drama coaches. Certainly there is nothing accidental about her management of the cabaret scene in *Bus Stop* as she struggles through 'That Old Black Magic', and there is something almost mystical about her ability to

Above left: as the bruised, bewitching Sugar in Some Like It Hot. *Above: the serene beauty of Marilyn Monroe – caught in a relaxed mood while filming* The Misfits

shift mood from low-comedy to the heart-touching pathos of which she was uniquely capable.

'I'm not interested in money,' she told a somewhat surprised early producer, 'I just want to be wonderful'. That ambition she achieved, triumphantly. DAVID ROBINSON

Filmography
1947 Dangerous Years. '48 Ladies of the Chorus. '49 Love Happy. '50 A Ticket to Tomahawk; The Asphalt Jungle; The Fireball; All About Eve; Right Cross. '51 Home Town Story; As Young As You Feel; Love Nest; Let's Make It Legal. '52 Clash by Night; We're Not Married; Don't Bother to Knock; Monkey Business; O. Henry's Full House *ep* The Cop and the Anthem (GB: Full House). '53 Niagara; Gentlemen Prefer Blondes; How to Marry a Millionaire. '54 River of No Return; There's No Business Like Show Business. '55 The Seven Year Itch. '56 Bus Stop. '57 The Prince and the Showgirl (GB). '59 Some Like It Hot. '60 Let's Make Love. '61 The Misfits. '62 Something's Got to Give (unfinished).

The Taming of Elizabeth Taylor

Audiences came to see Mickey Rooney in *National Velvet* and left talking instead about the young dark-haired beauty who played the winning rider. The dramas of Taylor's life far exceed the fictions of her screen roles. Much married (and maligned for it) the first of the million-dollar superstars continues to delight and amaze

On screen and off, changing her image and her husbands and descending into a defiantly overweight middle-age, Elizabeth Taylor has waged a continuing battle with her extraordinary beauty and fame. She has been expected to live up to the various images created for her by her studio, MGM, since she started making films as a child, and she has rebelled, timidly at first and then with increasing bravura. 'Rapturously beautiful', as James Agee described her in his review of *National Velvet* (1944), made when she was 12, she has had to work hard to prove that beneath the movie-star perfection she has character and wit and temperament.

Though for years she was the world's preeminent star, at the time the highest-paid performer in cinema history, she has never played a *grande dame* on film or appeared like one in her personal life. She has never been queenly – hence her odd, small and unexpectedly appealing performance as the Queen of the Nile in *Cleopatra* (1963). Her characters, for the most part, have sought love rather than power, have been palpably vulnerable and insecure rather than larger-than-life figures of great ambition and assurance. And yet, inevitably, the star's life that she has always led – the attention, the privileges and the often stinging personal and professional attacks launched against her – has left its mark. Despite her resistance to being 'Elizabeth Taylor', despite her evasions, her turnabouts in style and appearance, the fact that she has never had a normal life has made her seem, for all her warmth and earthiness, a little beyond human reach: she is a little mysterious, a little vague, as if she has her secrets; she suffers from a lingering self-consciousness and a touch (not of class, to be sure) of Hollywood artificiality.

Liz and marriage

Her spectacular private life could have been 'written' by someone who grew up on a steady diet of Hollywood melodramas. Keeping pace with her shifting movie images, her marriages seem to have caught her in different moods: as dewy *ingénue* (Mrs Nicky Hilton), dutiful childbride (Mrs Michael Wilding), boisterous highliver (Mrs Michael Todd), brazen homebreaker (Mrs Eddie Fisher) and passionate woman of the world (Mrs Richard Burton – twice). Currently, as Mrs John Warner, wife of the Republican Senator from Virginia, she has her most starlike role yet. Presiding over an estate in that state's lush hunt-country and hob-nobbing with politicians, she seems to be living a real-life version of the Southern belles she has played so often and with such flair. In the Elizabeth Taylor story, life and art mingle incestuously in a series of glittering counter-points and parallels.

On screen, as in her private life, she has not been content or able to settle into a single continuing role, but has moved ahead, trying out new ways of relating to the burdens of her beauty and fame. As child actress, adolescent, young woman, scarlet beauty and middle-aged shrew, she discovered a series of images

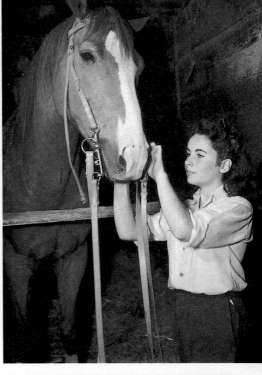

Left: Taylor as the ill-fated Southern belle in Raintree County. *Above: Taylor, Joan Bennett and Spencer Tracy as bride-to-be, mother and* Father of the Bride *(1950). Above right:* National Velvet *began Taylor's ascent to stardom. Right: the society girl with her lover (Montgomery Clift) in* A Place in the Sun. *Bottom: Maggie, the* Cat on a Hot Tin Roof, *with broken-legged, brooding, boozing husband (Paul Newman)*

that conformed to public expectation but also allowed her to reveal something of her private self as well. From angelic child to braying fishwife, her evolving image demonstrates a greater range than she is often credited with.

Innocence and experience

She was born in London in 1932 and evacuated with her parents to Hollywood at the outbreak of World War II. After a small role in Universal's *There's One Born Every Minute* (1941), she signed for MGM. Elizabeth Taylor the child star – of *Lassie Come Home, Jane Eyre* (both 1943) and *National Velvet* – had an ethereal quality that, viewed now in enlightened retrospect, is jarring. Sweet without being sticky, possessed of an almost mystical streak, her little girls were saintly characters. Her sculpted face, with her radiant, piercing eyes, had a grown-up's wisdom, and the young Elizabeth exuded a faintly unsettling preconscious sexuality. Her voice, high-pitched and breathy (as it has remained), also had a musical quality, and her remnants of an English accent lent her, in American settings, a dignified air. Strange to say, but as a child actress she had not a trace of vulgarity.

As she grew into adolescence and young womanhood, MGM did not quite know what to do with her dainty, refined, indeed almost otherworldly manner. She clearly was not a typical American teenager, and so she was cast as someone set apart from the American norm, like the society girl Angela Vickers in *A Place in the Sun* (1951).

Throughout the late Forties and early Fifties, Liz played little rich girls whose great wealth, or delicate physical condition, or luminous beauty, gave them special distinction. She is surprisingly serene and delicate and

always somewhat remote in these parts. But there were early indications, too, in *Little Women* (1949) for instance, that dainty Taylor had a sly sense of humour and a tongue that could sting; and throughout her la-de-dah *ingénue* period there were portents of the spitfire who blossomed in the mid-Fifties.

Broken-hearted belles

In *Giant* (1956), *Raintree County* (1957), *Cat on a Hot Tin Roof* (1958), *Suddenly, Last Summer* (1959) and *Butterfield 8* (1960), she was seen to act more visibly as she took on a series of wilful, high-spirited, sassy character parts (the last four earned her Oscar nominations in consecutive years). The upper-crust good manners of her young matrons were replaced by increasing doses of the common touch. Her style became harsher as she acquired manner and temperament, as brassiness and sarcasm chipped away at the inaccessible *ingénue* aura that she had never wanted. Interestingly, at the height of her beauty in films like *Raintree County* and *Cat on a Hot Tin Roof*, she played women spurned by men, women bruised and humiliated in the search for love. It is an image – Liz unlucky in love, the great beauty on the

romantic skids – that has stayed with her, off screen as well as on, and at least in movies has been subjected to increasingly baroque variations. Surely she is drawn to these cast-off mistresses and wives, these women tortured by romantic misfortunes, because they reflect aspects of her own insecurity, her very modest self-appraisal, her doubts about who she really is beneath the cosmetic star-packing.

Acknowledged as an actress and finally winning an Oscar, for *Butterfield 8*, Elizabeth Taylor dramatically embarked on a new phase to her career in the early Sixties: the main reasons were Richard Burton, *Cleopatra* and her elevation to superstardom. Her unprecedented million-dollar contracts and her private-life notoriety made it impossible for her to escape herself, and in hollow movies like *The VIPs* (1963) and *The Sandpiper* (1965), she was visibly and awkwardly self-conscious, once again a remote movie star playing fabricated movie-star roles. But her Oscar-winning performance in *Who's Afraid of Virginia Woolf?* (1966) saved her, giving her a new screen persona – one that she has, more or less, held on to ever since. The middle-aged strumpet she played released with full force the bitchy wit and Chaucerian bawdiness that had been struggling for expression in Liz since the time of *Giant*. With her rumbustious performance in *Who's Afraid of Virginia Woolf?* she became a fully fledged Hollywood dame, a West Coast version of the Wife of Bath, coarse, loud, earthy, blowzy and essentially good-hearted. Here was an image she clearly relished; at last she could forget about being beautiful or well-behaved – she was free to burlesque her earlier glamorous persona.

Since then, in films like *The Taming of the Shrew*, *Reflections in a Golden Eye* (both 1967), *Boom!* (1968), *Zee & Co* (1971) and *Hammersmith Is Out* (1972), she has conducted an ongoing rebellion against the blandness and containment of her earlier MGM image. And as her material has become quirkier and as she

has grown heavier and more shrill, she has seemed to enjoy being a movie star, perhaps for the first time. She has become something of a coterie performer, putting on a whale of a show for dedicated Elizabethans, mocking her sex-goddess, earth-mother image, delivering sarcastic dialogue with a swagger and flourish that the young actress could never have summoned. Her range narrowed, her technique became more mannered as she cultivated a battery of verbal tics – erratic phrasing, stammers, pauses, backtrackings, sudden whoops and dips in pitch and tone – but she acted with zest and abandon. This late, flamboyant phase of her career has a buoyancy, a sense of wicked self-mockery that is endearing.

A Taylor-made image

To many of her fans, the greying of Elizabeth Taylor may seem like the desecration of a national shrine, but to the lady herself it must be a relief to have her days of classic beauty safely behind her. Off screen, she has got herself up in jewellery and teased hair and gaudy tent-like dresses that seem like a parody of old Hollywood theatricality, and her essential good nature and sanity have emerged. Her latest image, with its Rabelaisian and Falstaffian echoes, seems like a final uncovering of her mask – she is letting us in on the uncorseted, fun-loving woman who has always been there beneath the star trappings, though perhaps the star herself has not always been aware of this.

She has certainly been vivid, but she has not had a good part in a good movie for many years. She was miscast, for example, in *A Little Night Music* (1977) because she does not have the diction, carriage or authority to play an autocratic stage actress. But she is still usable, a Hollywood trouper with a ripe personality – a former beauty who has turned herself into a skilful character actress with a wit and a style that are distinctly her own.

FOSTER HIRSCH

Above left: a glorious Cleopatra in the inglorious Cleopatra. *Bottom left: Burton and Taylor as tamer and tamed in* The Taming of the Shrew. *Above: the Burtons antagonizing each other in* Who's Afraid of Virginia Woolf? *Below: in* Zee & Co, *Susannah York (here with Taylor) plays the 'other woman' threatening an already shaky marriage*

Filmography

1941 There's One Born Every Minute. **'43** Lassie Come Home; Jane Eyre. **'44** The White Cliffs of Dover; National Velvet. **'46** Courage of Lassie. **'47** Cynthia (GB: The Rich Full Life); Life With Father. **'48** A Date With Judy; Julia Misbehaves. **'49** Little Women; Conspirator (GB). **'50** The Big Hangover; Father of the Bride. **'51** Father's Little Dividend; A Place in the Sun; Callaway Went That-a-Way (GB: The Star Said No); Love Is Better Than Ever (GB: The Light Fantastic). **'52** Ivanhoe (GB). **'53** The Girl Who Had Everything; Elephant Walk. **'54** Rhapsody; Beau Brummel; The Last Time I Saw Paris. **'56** Giant. **'57** Raintree County. **'58** Cat on a Hot Tin Roof. **'59** Suddenly, Last Summer; Scent of Mystery/Holiday in Spain. **'60** Butterfield 8. **'63** The VIPs (GB) (USA: International Hotel); Cleopatra. **'65** The Sandpiper. **'66** Who's Afraid of Virginia Woolf? **'67** The Taming of the Shrew (USA-IT); Reflections in a Golden Eye; The Comedians (USA-BERMUDA-FR). **'68** Dr Faustus (GB-IT); Boom! (GB); Secret Ceremony (GB). **'70** The Only Game in Town. **'71** Zee & Co (GB) (USA: X, Y and Zee); Under Milk Wood (GB). **'72** Hammersmith Is Out. **'73** Night Watch (GB); Ash Wednesday. **'74** That's Entertainment! (+ co-narr); Identikit (IT) (USA/GB: The Driver's Seat). **'76** The Blue Bird (USSR-USA). **'77** Victory at Entebbe; A Little Night Music (USA-A-GER). **'79** Winter Kills (uncredited). **'80** The Mirror Crack'd (GB).

Bad and Beautiful Lana Turner

term – 'Lanallure' – was coined to express the resultant commodity, and by the Sixties her films were sold very much on the basis of her clothes and 'look'. *Love Has Many Faces* (1965) boasted of its 'Million Dollar Wardrobe', and there even developed a certain kind of Lana dress style which heightened artifice by a use of man-made fibres and impractical designs. *The Bad and the Beautiful* (1952) plays on this element of her image: she portrays a movie star, showing the endless manufacture that goes into the production of her image.

To be glamorous is to be unreal, almost not human. What makes Lana Turner fascinating is that all this glamour is combined with her being so ordinary – and this too is characteristic of the Hollywood image industry. Here

Left: 'Lanallure' captured in a studio portrait by Eric Carpenter. Below: Lana Turner as the scheming wife who plots to murder her husband (Cecil Kellaway) in The Postman Always Rings Twice

Ordinary? She was beautiful, glamorous and filled a sweater with the best of them. Had these been all her attributes Lana Turner would have got on famously but an added attraction was a stunning catalogue of scandal which included numerous husbands, a few affairs and a corpse in the kitchen

To begin with, she is the epitome of Glamour. In Hollywood this is a certain set of qualities of a performer's own face and figure which are worked up into something else by the studios' glamour departments. Often it is hard to distinguish these two elements, but not so with Lana Turner. At the start of her career, her own qualities were used – a certain freshness and girlishness combined with a well-developed body and a face that looked as if the mind behind it dwelt continually on sex. In her

first film, *They Won't Forget* (1937), she had only to walk down the street of a small Southern town to enflame the local men so much that she ends up raped and murdered.

This could just be called sex-appeal. It is only really glamour when it begins to be packaged by the arts of makeup, hairdressing, costume, lighting and so on. Gradually, Lana's rather raw sex-appeal was wrapped up in the glossy, streamlined finish of the glamour merchants. So extreme did this become that a special

are these people leading fantastic lives, yet 'really' they are just like you and me. In Lana's case this is suggested by her most famous image – the 'sweater girl'. In this everyday garment she managed to be both ordinary and glamorous. Her early career provides a further illustration of the point. She rocketed to stardom – or so the publicity made it appear – after being 'discovered' at a soda fountain in a Hollywood drug store. Nor did she lose this 'common' touch. Many of her films capitalize on it – *Ziegfeld Girl* (1941) has her as a girl from the wrong side of the tracks who becomes a showgirl with the famous Ziegfeld Follies; *Cass Timberlane* (1947), with Spencer Tracy, is about a girl marrying above herself. Her ability to suggest simplicity gives a special frisson to her murderous role in *The Postman Always Rings Twice* (1946), and carries her through some of

Top left: a brunette Lana (left) in They Won't Forget *with Gloria Dickson. Top:* Ziegfeld Girl *featured (from left to right) Anya Tarrande, Lana, Hedy Lamarr and Judy Garland. Above: made in 1941,* Honky Tonk *is the story of a Western con-man who meets his match. Left: Lana in the 1948 version of* The Three Musketeers *with Gene Kelly*

the artifices of the later films.

Yet this duality also relates to another point: the corruption of ordinariness by those very qualities of sex-appeal and glamour. Lana's life is a stunning catalogue of scandal. Married ten times (to nine men), often under dubious circumstances, there were also many charges of nymphomania, drunkenness, suicide attempts, home-wrecking, plus the number one scandal when an affair she was having with a small-time gigolo/crook, Johnny Stompanato, was brought to an abrupt halt when he was stabbed to death one storm-filled night in her kitchen. At the subsequent trial Lana's daughter Cheryl was convicted, and Cheryl was to figure – as the classic delinquent daughter of rich America variously accused of drug-taking, lesbianism and being a professional stripper – in Lana's later image.

Few film stars can boast a 'private' life quite so rich in incident as this, and it is almost as if her life is itself a moral fiction – an evocation of the wonderful world of wealth to which American culture aspires, and a demonstration of the vicissitudes it brings with it. These resonances carry over into the films. *Peyton Place* (1957) was, by chance, released when the Stompanato trial was underway, and involves a courtroom performance that many have likened to her behaviour at her daughter's trial. *Imitation of Life* (1959), which could be the title of Lana's own biography, involves a sub-plot of her daughter falling in love with her boyfriend – a state of affairs which was read into the Stompanato incident. More than these specific correspondences, the films also celebrate wealth, or else expose its corruption in a series of plots and situations that echo and

rework Lana's image. *Peyton Place*, the well-to-do small town with a seething underside of sensuality; *Imitation of Life*, a story of the seediness and hollowness of the aspirations and achievements of success; *Latin Lovers* (1953), about the 'wealthiest woman in the world' who cannot, therefore, find true love – and so on.

This is all fabulous and salacious by turns, but Lana's presence also makes it accessible, something anyone can identify with. Significantly, whereas as a young star her major fans were men, later on she became an identification figure for women fans. This is partly the vicarious pleasure to be had from watching ordinary Lana swanning about in minks and freely indulging her sexuality. But there is a further twist – suffering. Throughout her career there has been a stress on suffering – the

Opposite page: Lana in The Prodigal *(1955). Bottom left: with Robert Taylor in* Johnny Eager *(1941). Centre: in* Love Has Many Faces *(1965) with Cliff Robertson. Left: with Lorne Greene in* Peyton Place. *Above: between takes for* Diane *(1955)*

sexuality . . . the consequent scandals . . . the broken marriages. The films reflect this, especially at their most vividly realized climaxes – her drunken collapse during the final number of *Ziegfeld Girl*, her hysterical drive in the rain when she discovers her lover has another woman in *The Bad and the Beautiful*, her terrible grief-stricken moment at the bedside of her best friend in *Imitation of Life*, the trial scene in *Peyton Place*. These are the moments at which the gloss of glamour is shed, and raw suffering is conveyed.

So there is a double movement – celebration of aspirations, revelation of the unhappiness attendant on it. Why should this have produced such a following among women? Impossible to know for sure, but it perhaps performed a time-honoured Hollywood job – both giving the people the pleasure of something beyond the dreariness of their actual lives, and yet in the end confirming them in the rightness of those actual lives, given the prices they have to pay for something better. And no one conveyed that double message better than Lana . . . on or off the screen.

RICHARD DYER

Filmography
1937 They Won't Forget; A Star Is Born; The Great Garrick. **'38** The Adventures of Marco Polo; Love Finds Andy Hardy; The Chaser; Rich Man, Poor Girl; Dramatic School. **'39** Calling Dr Kildare; These Glamour Girls; Dancing Co-Ed. **'40** Two Girls on Broadway; We Who Are Young. **'41** Ziegfeld Girl; Dr Jekyll and Mr Hyde; Honky Tonk; Johnny Eager. **'42** Somewhere I'll Find You. **'43** The Youngest Profession; DuBarry Was a Lady. **'44** Marriage Is a Private Affair. **'45** Keep Your Powder Dry; Weekend at the Waldorf. **'46** The Postman Always Rings Twice. **'47** Green Dolphin Street; Cass Timberlane. **'48** Homecoming; The Three Musketeers. **'50** A Life of Her Own. **'51** Mr Imperium. **'52** The Merry Widow; The Bad and the Beautiful. **'53** Latin Lovers. **'54** The Flame and the Flesh; Betrayed. **'55** The Prodigal; The Sea Chase. **'56** The Rains of Ranchipur; Diane. **'57** Peyton Place; The Lady Takes a Flyer. **'58** Another Time, Another Place. **'59** Imitation of Life. **'60** Portrait in Black. **'61** By Love Possessed; Bachelor in Paradise. **'62** Who's Got the Action? **'65** Love Has Many Faces. **'66** Madame X. **'69** The Big Cube (USA-MEXICO). **'74** Persecution/ Sheba/The Terror of Sheba (GB). **'76** Bittersweet Love.

BIG BAD MAE

'Virtue has its own reward but no sale at the box office'

About two-thirds of the way through a quite unremarkable gangland drama, a new character suddenly enters, swaying easily and provocatively into a swank speakeasy. She leaves her coat, and as she removes it there is a glint of diamonds. The checkroom girl, impressed, remarks: 'Goodness, what beautiful diamonds.' 'Goodness had nothing to do with it, dearie,' replies Mae West, and sways on up the stairs into screen history. The film is *Night After Night*, the date 1932.

Even at this time she was no newcomer to show business. She was, according to her own estimate, pushing 40 (others put the year of her birth back from 1893 to 1886), and had been on stage in various ways since the age of six. She had played all the 'littles' (Little Lord Fauntleroy, Little Eva) in repertory, been billed as the 'Baby Vamp', originated the 'shimmy', been a top star in vaudeville, and since 1926 had been a phenomenon of the legitimate stage in a series of plays written by herself. These included the luridly titled *Sex, Diamond Lil, Pleasure Man*, and *The Constant Sinner*. The contents had been scarcely less alarming: one of her plays, *The Drag*, about a group of homosexuals, never reached New York for fear of puritan wrath, and *Pleasure Man* was the subject of a famous court hearing on the grounds of obscenity – which, let it be said, Mae West won.

She was good at winning out in such situations. And rightly so. She made sex a joke, which, though it may not be the only reasonable way of looking at it, was at least a lot better than pretending it did not exist unless it was disguised as 'romance', which was, of course, sacred to every shopgirl and never involved anything nasty unless it was immediately paid for in the worst possible way. But Mae kept everyone guessing. Her stream of snappy and outrageous innuendoes could never quite be pinned down or brought to book by public moralists. Even in New York theatre in the Twenties, she stood almost alone in her defence of sex against the repressive forces of puritanism. A rush of prosecutions in 1928 led to the introduction of an official code of morals for drama which set back freedom of speech in the theatre by several decades. This new era of restriction was, perhaps, a measure of America's increasing self-consciousness about where it stood in the modern cultivated world once it had left bold, bawdy pioneering days behind.

'It's not the men in my life that counts – it's the life in my men'

If so, Hollywood, with much less conscious yearning after culture, still lagged behind. The movement to clean up the movies was still hanging fire, and the freedom of speech and action allowed in the early talkies was surprising. Mae West was the perfect person to exploit it – and she did so with entirely fetching verve and good humour. To begin with, she was herself a parody of sex. If there was ever an era in her early career when she could have passed muster as a serious sex siren, the surviving

Left: Mae, shortly after arriving in Hollywood in 1932, in a publicity shot for Night After Night

The lady is a vamp – Mae around 1910 (left); the heavily censored Belle of the Nineties *(below left);* I'm No Angel *(above); Mae's screen debut,* Night After Night *(right)*

photographs do not show much evidence of it. By the time she made her first film she was already middle-aged and her always generous curves had filled out to a more than Junoesque amplitude; her rather pudgy features were made up in what was already an anachronistic fashion with a Cupid's-bow mouth and much eye-shadow and mascara. This was emphatically *not* the dutiful wife and mother image, nor was it a frontier woman – unless by the artificial light of a Western saloon. The effect was enhanced by her avoidance of modern dress: whenever possible she was decked out in the feathers and flounces of the Gay Nineties, and even when it was not possible she still somehow managed to leave that impression. Not only did goodness have nothing to do with it, nature had precious little to do with it either.

'I used to be Snow White – but I drifted'

And yet the overall tone of her films – the scripts of which she always wrote, largely or wholly, herself – was of a breezy realism, at least about the basic facts of life. She was funny too. A natural clown, deflating pomposity and self-importance, making fun of herself and what she seemed to represent in terms of outrageous sexual promise, she dominated every film she made and emerged as one of the cinema's great originals. Even Mae's belated appearance in *Night After Night* took over the film completely. She was already writing her own dialogue and ordering the director around; she felt she knew what was best for herself – and the world agreed with her. As a result of the sensation she caused with this film she was given a free hand with the next, and produced one of the most important and successful pictures of the decade. *She Done Him Wrong* (1933) financially saved the ailing Paramount studios, to whom she was under contract, from having to sell out to MGM. The

film was an adaptation of her play *Diamond Lil,* which suffered a title change because of its theatrical notoriety but was otherwise left alone – a cheerfully amoral tale of a lady of easy virtue, the men in her life, and the way that everything obstructing her is shunted aside to leave her completely on top and without a shade of guilt.

'Any time you got nothing to do – and lots of time to do it, come on up'

From here, with the public screaming for more, she went straight into perhaps her most extravagant role, as a nightclub singer who is also a glamorous lady lion-tamer, in *I'm No Angel* (1933). The picture was based on a script by Lowell Brentano, entirely reworked, as usual, by Mae West to conform with her characterization and its requirements. For like all the screen's great comedians, she essentially played the same role in all her films. And if, at first, it was not herself she was playing, it rapidly became a pretty good approximation. Even so it is noticeable that there has always been a clear separation between Mae West the person and Mae West the product: she tends to talk, in regard to her films, of how 'Mae West would not do this, might do that' rather than in the first person. And as she was the creator of this personage, so she was really the *auteur* of her films – on those occasions when she was not, they fell below past standards.

'Is that a gun in your pocket, or are you just glad to see me?'

Evidently she hit it off very well with Lowell Sherman, director of *She Done Him Wrong,* and Wesley Ruggles, director of *I'm No Angel,* but much less so, it seems, with Leo McCarey, who directed her third vehicle, *Belle of the Nineties*

In She Done Him Wrong *Mae resists Owen Moore (above) but later tells Cary Grant to 'Come up sometime, see me'. Klondike Annie (top) was brutally cut after complaints by women's groups. My Little Chickadee (top right), which was not a great box-office success, was the only film to co-star Mae and W.C. Fields, whose heavy drinking she frowned upon*

(1934). McCarey had his own ideas about how to put together a film comedy, and these frequently did not coincide with Mae's. This may well be one of the reasons for the film's relative feebleness compared with the previous two. Also it is another, lesser version of *Diamond Lil* (to be followed in 1936 by another, the even lesser *Klondike Annie*). But most damaging, no doubt, was the tightening up in 1934 of the Hays Office regulations regarding morality in films; everything touching on sex in movies became subject to scrutiny under this organization's notorious code with its petty, finely graduated rules and restrictions. *Belle of the Nineties* was the first of Mae's films

to be seriously interfered with in production. Both plot and dialogue were censored, and the title had to be changed from the more challenging *It Ain't No Sin*. It was still a big success with the public, but the golden era of Mae West in movies was past. Her next film, *Goin' to Town* (1935), had moments of memorable lunacy – in the craziest plot of all her films she is a cattle rustler's widow who breaks into high society and sings an aria from *Samson and Delilah* along the way – but from then on it was downhill. Even a screen encounter with W.C. Fields, in *My Little Chickadee* (1940), fell rather flat.

The reasons for this decline seem to be intimately bound up with censorship. A lot of her humour is very direct and, in a way, naive. It depends on statement and absolutely unavoidable inference. What could, and did, provoke a belly laugh becomes (when forced to go undercover and be slyly circumspect) either totally colourless and innocuous or else smutty. The necessity to be devious took away Mae West's most effective weapon, and she

was never happy without the power to say what she meant – and leave no doubts.

MAE: I like sophisticated men
    to take me out
MAN: I'm not
    really sophisticated
MAE: You're not
    really out yet either

Strangely, this decline did little or nothing to reduce Mae West's status as a legend. Of course, she continued working in other media – radio in the mid-Thirties, the theatre again in the late Forties with *Catherine Was Great* and revivals of *Diamond Lil*, and cabaret in Las Vegas in the Fifties. *The Heat's On* (1943), her next film, was neither here nor there, though she did look extraordinary in it. Her 'comeback' in *Myra Breckinridge* (1970) was hardly more than a guest appearance. And her latest film, *Sextette* (1978), is bizarre beyond belief, with this lady of 85 (or maybe 92) as the centre of amorous intrigue, lusted after by half a dozen men young enough, in a couple of cases, to be her great-grandsons. And yet somehow it does not matter. She is still Mae West, and the Mae West of today is only marginally more of a fantasy than the Mae West of 50 years ago. She was and is her own creation, and as such gave something unique to the cinema – herself. If the censors ruined her screen career, they also helped her towards immortality.

JOHN RUSSELL TAYLOR

Filmography
1932 Night After Night. '33 She Done Him Wrong; I'm No Angel (+sc). '34 Belle of the Nineties (+sc). '35 Goin' to Town (+sc). '36 Klondike Annie (+sc); Go West, Young Man (+sc). '38 Every Day's a Holiday (+sc). '40 My Little Chickadee (+co-sc). '43 The Heat's On (GB: Tropicana). '70 Myra Breckinridge. '78 Sextette.